HAKA!

HAKA!

TE TOHU O TE WHENUA RANGATIRA
The Dance of a Noble People

TĪMOTI KĀRETU

REED

Reed Publishing (NZ) Ltd
Te Karuhi tā tāpui o Reed (Aotearoa)

Established in 1907, Reed is New Zealand's largest
book publisher, with over 300 titles in print.

For details on all these books visit our website:
www.reed.co.nz

First published 1993 by Reed Books, a division of Reed Publishing (NZ) Ltd,
39 Rawene Road, Birkenhead, Auckland 10. Associated companies, branches and
representatives throughout the world.

Reprint 1994, 1996, 2000, 2001, 2002, 2005
Copyright @ Timoti Kāretu 1993

National Library of New Zealand
Cataloguing-in-Publication data

Kāretu, T.S. (Tīmoti Sam), 1937-
Haka : te tohu o te whenua rangatira / Tīmoti Kāretu.
1 v.
ISBN 0-7900-0290-6
1. Haka (Dance) 2. Maori (New Zealand people) -- Social life
and customs. I. Title.
793.31993 (306.089994) zbn93-044501

Design by Claire Preen
Printed in New Zealand

He whakamaumaharatanga
ki a
Tā Kīngi Matutaera Īhaka
Moe mai, e Matu.

To the memory of
Sir Kīngi Matutaera Īhaka

CONTENTS

HE MIHI

ACKNOWLEDGEMENTS

Ehara taku toa i te toa takitahi engari ia he toa takitini.

Āe, nā te takimaha i oti ai ngā kōrero nei, arā, nā rātou kua takoto i te urunga tē taka, kua karapinepine atu ki te kāpunipunitanga o te wairua. Heoi anō rā ko koutou, te hunga whakatutū puehu o runga i ngā marae o ngā tau ka hipa, ki a koutou.

He rongonga kupu, he hokinga whakaaro. Ka rongo au i ngā kupu o ētahi o ngā haka e whakahuatia ake nei ka hoki ngā mahara ki a koutou i tohutohu, i riri, i āwhina, i whakanui nei i a au i te wā o te pūhoutanga. Ka eke nei ki te karangatanga taipakeke ka hoki nga whakaaro, ka tangi taku mapu, ka kī ki a au anō, āe taku waimarie i mōhio au ki a koutou Moe mai, moe mai.

Ka huri ake ki te ao tūroa ka rere aku mihi ki te hunga i tuku nei kia patapataihia rātou e au, arā, ki te mōrehu kaumātua o Ngāti Whakaue, ki a Hāmuera Mitchell, ki a Tā Kīngi Matutaera Īhaka, ki a Ngāpo Wehi, kaitātaki, kaiwhakaako o Wakahuia; ki a Horowaewae Maxwell, kaitātaki, kaiwhakaako o Rangiwewehi; ki a huhua noa o roto i nga kapa haka o te motu.

Ki ngā kaipatopato mai i ngā kōrero nei, arā aku hēkeretari a Hinetapuarau Ioane o Te Whānau-a-Apanui, a Hine-ki-waiaua Hōri rāua ko Miriama Kingi ōku anō nei, ka nui te mihi atu. Ehara i te mahi māmā, engari ia he takeo, he hokehokeā.

Ka rere anō he mihi ki a Mātene Rūāwai, rātou ko Hēni Jacob, ko Wareko Te Angina, ko Rowland McLeod i whakamahia nei e au kia pānui i ngā kōrero nei kia kitea noa ihotia ai mena e mārama ana, e maroke rawa ana rānei! Kāore rātou i mataku ki te kī mai pēhea, pēhea!

Me kore ake te whare pukapuka o Te Whare Wānanga o Waikato ki te kimi mai i ngā kōrero hei āta pānui, hei āta tirotiro māku. Nō reira, ki a Jenny King, ki te rangatira o te whare pukapuka, me tō raro tonu mai i a ia, ki a Tony Millett nāna nei te rārangi pukapuka i whakarite, i whakatika, tae atu hoki ki ā rāua kaimahi, tēnā rā koutou katoa.

Ko ngā nakonakotanga, arā, ko ngā whakaahua o ngā kapa o ēnei rā nei nā Vince Hēperi, ā, ko ērā o ngā tau maha ki muri nō roto mai i te kohikohinga whakaahua a te whare pukapuka o Alexander Turnbull. E ngā kaiwhakanakonako, i kitea ai te ātaahua o tēnei mahi, o te haka, me mihi rā.

Ko aku mihi whakamutunga ki taku kapa o Te Whare Wānanga o Waikato ko rātou nei ki te whakatinana i ngā kupu i titoa ai e au ahakoa waiata, waiata-ā-ringa, haka rānei. Nā rātou i puta ai ngā kupu a Tīmoti ki te ao hei whakarongo mā te taringa, hei puhipuhi mā te hau.

9

Hei whakatepe noa ake me nui te mihi ki taku tuakana, ki a Te Wharehuia Milroy, i rite tonu nei taku whakapōrearea atu i a ia kia kī mai āe rānei, kāore rānei i te tau, i te pai, i te hāngai aku kupu. I tua atu i a ia ko ngā kaitātaki o taku kapa ko Te Rita Papesch rāua ko Hōhepa Harawira, i ū nei ki aku tohutohu ahakoa te kore e rata mai, te whakaae mai. Ka mihi rā te ngākau, ka mihi rā.

Kāti, nei rā tā tātou taonga ka tukua nei ki te ao. Wai ka hua, wai ka tohu ka pēheatia mai, kei a koutou tēnā.

I oti ai, i tutuki ai nā rau ringa, nō reira ka mihi tonu, ka mihi tonu, tēnā koutou katoa.

HE KUPU WHAKATAKI

INTRODUCTION

KO TE HAKA HE TOHU WHENUA RANGATIRA

Apart from the five years I spent at Wellington College where I refused to perform the bowdlerised versions of Utaina (the boarders' haka) and Ka Mate (the haka of the whole school), I do not recall a time when I was not actively involved in haka. From Kōkako Māori School and Waimako marae in Waikaremoana to Waimārama Māori School, twenty miles east of Hastings; from Wellington Teachers' College and Victoria University of Wellington to Te Rangatahi in Taumarunui to Ngāti Rānana in London, England; from He Toa Takitini to Te Iti Kahurangi to Tūhoe ki Waikato to Te Whare Wānanga o Waikato in Hamilton.

My involvement in haka over these years has been as performer, tutor, composer, critic and adjudicator. During that time I met, and was influenced and instructed by, many of the experts in the field.

Our tutor at Waimako marae was Mac Moses, a very benevolent despot, but more often than not we watched the adults and emulated their movements. Every day at school there was time devoted to haka, poi, waiata-ā-ringa and waiata. In Waimārama the haka master was my grand-uncle Taki Winitana. He was marvellous to watch and exciting to perform with. I always used to think his eyes were on permanent putē and permanent pūkana!

At Wellington Teachers' College and Victoria University we were very much on our own and were taught by fellow students quite often not knowing whether we were correct or not. In retrospect, I feel we did no justice to such haka as Rūaumoko, Ko Ranginui te Atua, and others.

There was an intercollegiate competition among the teachers' colleges on haka and allied arts, and the year we hosted the competition, 1958, one of the judges was the late Venerable Archdeacon Sir Kīngi Īhaka, not then a knight. We were peremptorily dismissed by him but, to this day, I remember his comments which have stood me in good stead.

1960 was my first year of full employment at Taumarunui High School and I was asked to tutor a group called Te Rangatahi. I learnt more from them than they did from me, the haka man par excellence in the group being the late Bob Jones along with two women from Te Arawa — Huia Jones (Bob's wife), and Maramena Rauhina, known affectionately to all as Babs. I have very fond memories of this group, who treated me with a deference which was well in excess of that deserved.

At the end of 1961 I travelled to London and assumed the position of Information Officer at the New Zealand High Commission. The group now known as Ngāti Rānana was just newly formed and, again, I was asked to be tutor. Many of the performers had never performed before their sojourn in London but what was lacking in experience was more than compensated for by enthusiasm.

Upon returning to Aotearoa in early 1969 and assuming a position at Fairfield College, Hamilton, I met the late Canon Wī Te Tau Huata, tutor and mentor of He Toa Takitini.

At the coronation celebrations in 1969 of Te Ariki Nui, Dame Te Ata-i-rangi-kaahu, Canon Huata asked me to be one of the adjudicators for the competitions in haka that formed part of the celebrations. It was only the second time I had adjudicated, the first being before the coronation celebrations at Tauranga where I had been inveigled into adjudicating by the late Hārata Papesch and Hera Munro, now Hera Blyde. Of the adjudicating panel at Tauranga I was the neophyte but I was in very august company — Hāmuera Mitchell, Tenga Rangitauira, Hārata Papesch, Hera Blyde, George Brennan. It was these people who, initially, encouraged me to adjudicate and who gave me the benefit of their experience. Before adjudicating at the coronation celebrations we were assembled by Piri Poutapu, master carver and haka tutor, who instructed us in the finer points of adjudicating. Much of what he had to say still rings in my ears.

In 1970 there was a royal tour and tribal areas were asked to provide groups of no fewer than a hundred people. Waikato-Maniapoto rallied to the call with Canon Huata composing the material and he and I being the tutors of the group. The big Māori welcome to the royal family took place in Gisborne.

1972 was an eventful year for two reasons. It was the year of the inaugural New Zealand Polynesian Festival, now known as The Aotearoa Māori Performing Arts Festival, held at Whakarewarewa, Rotorua, and I participated in that festival with He Toa Takitini under the aegis of Canon Huata. Secondly, Māori Language Day was introduced, an initiative of Ngā Tama Toa and Māori students at tertiary institutions. To celebrate the occasion, a public performance of haka and song was held at the Founders' Theatre in Hamilton. One of the groups participating was Te Iti Kahurangi, a group of more mature performers, tutored by me. This was to be the group that welcomed visitors to the official opening of the meeting-house Tūwaerea of Hui-te-rangi-ora marae, Hamilton, in 1974, and in 1975 welcomed the delegates to the annual conference of the Māori Women's Welfare League.

1973 was the first year that students of Māori language and culture at Waikato University went on a field trip to a marae to observe protocol in action and also to put their language skills to active use. Part of the preparation for these trips was to learn haka, chant and waiata-ā-ringa.

It was the students of these trips who became the nucleus of Te Whare Wānanga o Waikato culture group, which has been tutored by me since 1977, the year it came into being.

In the meantime I have continued to adjudicate at the annual celebrations of the coronation of Te Ariki Nui, at secondary schools festivals, at festivals of my own tribe, Tūhoe, at regional competitions and also in Australia.

In 1969 at the home of Canon Huata I met Te Hokowhitu-a-Tū concert party led by the charismatic, warm personality of Ngoi Pēwhairangi who was to be one of the greatest influences on me with regard to adjudication, composition and language. She was to retain that influence right up to her untimely death in 1985. I also met in 1969, on an adjudication panel in Hastings, Ērana Coulter, another lady with strong opinions about haka and a very beautiful performer. She died tragically in a car accident in 1984.

Perhaps the strongest influence on me in this whole field of haka was John Te Rangiāniwaniwa Rangihau, whose very name would worry some groups when they heard he was to be one of the adjudicating panel. Very much an uncompromising traditionalist, he was my chief mentor and critic. In 1980, when Te Whare Wānanga o Waikato travelled to Tahiti, Hawaii and the mainland USA, he came as our kaumātua. In Tahiti he performed with us and it was probably his last public performance. A master of the mere, taiaha and the word, he was known throughout the whole of the Māori world.

The aforementioned names have been the reason for my continued interest in haka. Many of these people, whose influence on me was so strong, are no longer with us. Memories come flooding back as I recite each name and recall the circumstances under which we argued, debated, cajoled, wheedled. I doubt that I had anything to offer them but the riches they gave me are incalculable.

Each generation changes and what one did not accept another does. As conventions and philosophies of haka are ignored for the sake of applause and victory, so the whole art becomes shallow. The exaggerated stance, the multiplicity of movements, the needless jumping, the concentration on the peripheral to the detriment of the essential I find untenable in the light of the teachings of those who have passed on but who gave me their time, their experience, their expertise, and their aroha. It is in remembrance of them, and for the sake of haka, that one persists and perseveres.

The language will continue to be the difficult issue for most of the young performers but for haka to be meaningful and to survive the young performer must know what is being said, how to interpret what is being said and how to imbue that interpretation with passion and panache. Not to do so, is to do haka and our ancestors an injustice.

No Māori ceremony is complete without haka. It is as fundamental to our rites of passage as the language and is the reason why this book was contemplated. More importantly though it is my paean of praise and gratitude to my mentors who have passed on, and to my mentors still living. Tēnā rā koutou katoa.

To the many no longer with us I say,

    'Ngaro noa aku tau i te huakanga ata
    Te whakarewatanga mai i te tara ki Maumahara
    Pākinikini ai te mamae
    Māringiringi ai te wai i te kamo
    I te kai kino a aroha
    Kei aku puna o te kī, kei taku tahuna-ā-tara
    Te haruru tonu nei ā koutou kupu
    Te haruru tonu nei ō koutou tapuwae
    I muri nei
    Taiaha hā! Taiaha hā!

    Gone are my loved ones at break of day
    As it comes over the summit of Maumahara
    Pain gnaws away within,
    Tears flow unrestrained
    Because of the emotion I feel
    My orators, composers without peer
    You my assembly of chiefs
    Your words still resound
    Your footsteps are still heard
    Long after you have gone
    Taiaha hā! Taiaha hā!'

To the generations to come I say,

    'Nei rā ō puipuiaki, ō tongarerewa
    Rauhītia! Maimoatia!
    Engari kei noho koe
    Ka tuku kia mate!

    Yours is an illustrious heritage
    Cherish it, nurture it
    but never ever
    Let it die!'

Tihē mauri ora!

HAKA AND LEGEND

Māori myth and tribal histories abound with reference to the haka.

TINIRAU AND KAE

The first kapa haka (haka troupe) of Māoridom is said to be the women of Tinirau whose principal function was to find and destroy Kae who had slain and eaten Tutunui, the tame whale of Tinirau.

Tinirau had permitted Kae to return to his home on the back of Tutunui. Upon arrival Kae refused to dismount and the whale, in its endeavours to unseat Kae, became stranded and was killed and eaten by Kae. Tinirau awaited the return of his pet but because of the delay came to the conclusion that some calamity had befallen Tutunui. Tinirau eventually realised that Kae had killed and eaten Tutunui.

Tinirau then called together his best women performers and sent them off to capture Kae and bring him to Tinirau. None of the women knew Kae but were told that they would recognise him by the gap in his teeth. To be able to do that, they would have to cause him to laugh and it was felt that a troupe of women could achieve that more easily than a troupe of men. The troupe comprised some of the best known figures of Māori tradition, Hine-te-iwaiwa, Rau-kata-uri, Rau-kata-mea, Rūhirūhi, Hine-te-otaota, Hine-mārekareka and others, all personified forms of various aspects of the dance.

They set about their task of entertaining the people with enthusiasm and concluded their very entertaining performance with a haka. The haka was so effective that it caused Kae to laugh, thus exposing the gap in his teeth.

By means of appropriate incantation Kae was rendered unconscious and returned by the women to their home, where he was killed by Tinirau, thereby avenging the death of his pet whale Tutunui.

This is the haka they performed:

E ako au ki te haka
E ako au ki te ringaringa
E ako au ki te whewhera
E kāore te whewhera
E ako au ki te kōwhiti
E kāore te kōwhiti
E kōwhiti nuku, e kōwhiti rangi
E kōwhiti puapua, e kōwhiti werewere
E hanahana a tinaku . . . e![1]

I learn to haka
I learn to explore with my hands
I learn to open wide
Not to open wide
I learn to twitch
Not to twitch
Pulsating upwards, pulsating downwards
My vagina throbs, my vagina fibrillates
A haven of lingering warmth.

MĀUI-TIKITIKI-O-TARANGA

In the story of Māui-tikitiki-o-Taranga's attempts to locate his parents during the hours of daylight, his first encounter with his older brothers is while they are performing the haka. It is at the end of this performance that Taranga, Māui's natural mother, realises that the son she thought was dead is still alive and acknowledges him publicly for the first time.

TAMA-TE-KAPUA AND WHAKATŪRIA

Tama-te-kapua, captain of Te Arawa canoe and his younger brother, Whakatūria, are apprehended by the people of Uenuku, high chief of Hawaiki, after having stolen his breadfruit. Tama-te-kapua and Whakatūria use stilts in their theft but are caught. Tama-te-kapua is fortunate enough to elude his captors but his brother is strung up to the ceiling of the meeting house and left there to suffer the effects of the smoke rising from the fire.

Tama-te-kapua climbs onto the roof of the house and makes a hole just above where his brother is suspended. Together they devise a way to help Whakatūria escape. Whakatūria watches his captors rehearsing haka and taunts them for their incompetence. He boasts to them that he is a better dancer and that he is prepared to demonstrate. He asks to be permitted to wash the smoke from his body, to adorn himself appropriately for the dance and to be given a hand weapon to help accentuate the movements in the haka. This is agreed to. Whakatūria begins to haka and it is soon apparent that he is, indeed, an excellent performer. The captors are mesmerised by his performance and after moving around the house Whakatūria asks them if they might not agree to having the front door open to allow him to cool after his exertions.

Once the door is open Whakatūria resumes his performance. Eventually he makes his way towards the entrance and slips out. Tama-te-kapua is waiting for him, and together they pull the door to, lock it and the windows, and run off to safety.

TE PONGA AND TE PUHI-HUIA

It is not too difficult to imagine the mutual attraction that can be generated between performers when they are in full cry and giving their all.

Legend has a geat deal of evidence to support this thesis. The haka
plays an important role, too, in the story of Te Ponga and Te Puhi-huia
for it is during the performance of the haka that each feels the stirrings
of attraction for the other.

There had been constant battling between the people of Awhitū of
Manukau Harbour and the people of Maungawhau, known today as Mt
Eden, with each side claiming victory on occasion. The people of
Awhitū, with their chief Te Ponga, decide that it is time peace was
declared between the two factions. With this intent Te Ponga and his
people set out for Maungawhau.

They are welcomed with all appropriate ceremony and food in abun-
dance is served. However, the guests decide not to consume too much
lest their performance that evening be marred by over-eating. As dusk
settles both host and guest await the evening's performances with anti-
cipation and impatience. Eventually, the entertainment begins with
each group alternating.

Meanwhile, Te Puhi-huia, the daughter of the chief of Maungawhau,
is biding her time as to when she should make her entrance into the
performance. She does not yet wish to stand in front of the front rank
of the group but rather just be a member of it while she assesses the situation.

The appropriate moment for her to make her entrance soon arrives
and she begins to dance. Te Puhi-huia's movements are so beautiful she
is compared to the appearance of the moon on the twelfth night rising
above the horizon. The guests are enthralled and Te Ponga loses his
heart to her.

Te Ponga now feels that he, too, would like to display his prowess in
the dance and like Te Puhi-huia waits for the appropriate time to do so.
At last it arrives and Te Ponga appears, displaying his masculine
beauty and his competence in the dance. The audience are equally
enthralled by his performance.

Later, when all have returned to their quarters, Te Puhi-huia is left to
admit to her strong feelings for Te Ponga. She decides to reveal her
feelings to the object of her affections but is uncertain as to how she
should do so and yet maintain a sense of decorum, as she is the daughter of the chief.

Te Ponga and Te Puhi-huia are now hopelessly in love with each
other but neither has yet revealed so to the other. It is Te Ponga's slave
who suggests that he feign thirst and not accept a drink from the slaves.
Te Puhi-huia, to uphold the mana of her people, is forced to serve Te
Ponga herself and it is on this occasion that each confesses to being in
love with the other.

TE KAHUREREMOA AND TAKA-KŌPIRI
The story of Te Kahureremoa and Taka-kōpiri has a similar theme.

Te Kahureremoa, daughter of Paka, high chief of Wharekawa, in the Hauraki Gulf, is chided by her father for committing a social blunder and in her shame she and her slave leave their home to seek out Taka-kōpiri, chief of Katikati, near Tauranga, to whom she is strongly attracted.

She arrives at Katikati, and finds Taka-kōpiri's people, Waitaha, there. In recognition of her high status the people congregate on the marae to welcome her. After the rituals of welcome, food is served and by the time the meal is over night has fallen. The fires in the house are stoked and everyone settles down for the evening's performance of song and dance. The people wait and hope that their performance will motivate and encourage Kahureremoa to dance.

After some time has elapsed, Kahureremoa looks about her and then rises to perform. As the Māori text says:

Tino whakatikanga o te wahine nei ki runga ki te haka i te toronga kautanga o ngā ringa inamata e whakatangihia ana ki te ngongoro ko ngā ringa me te mea ka marere, ko ngā koikara piri ana i tua i te angaangamate o te kapu o te ringa koia anō me te mea e komu-rua ana te tamāhine a Paka, tā te Aitanga-a-Tiki pai, tā te kotahi a Tū-tawake pai, arā ōna whakataukī o te rangatira, 'He riri anō tā te tawa uho, he riri anō tā te tawa para arā ō te rangatira, ōna whakataukī, tū atu ki te haka, he haka anō tā te rangatira, he haka anō tā te ware, he porahu noa iho ngā ringa . . .

And so the woman rises to dance, as soon as she extends her arms exclamations of surprise and admiration can be heard it is as though her hands will leave her body, her fingers arch to touch the back of her hands; it is as though the suppleness of Paka's daughter has come from constant training and massage, she is the epitome of feminine grace and beauty in the dance; there are many sayings concerning the nobility, the sound tawa has its qualities, the inferior tawa has its qualities so it is said of the high born when they rise to haka that they have their style and the low-born have theirs, their hands look awkward.[2]

Kahureremoa's performance has hypnotised the chief, Taka-kōpiri, and he becomes strongly attracted to her as a consequence. Eventually they are united.

WAIRANGI

Parewhete, senior wife of Wairangi, commits adultery with the visiting chief, Tūpeteka. The fact is duly reported to Wairangi by one of his other wives in a fit of pique. Wairangi, in his anger, strikes his wife Parewhete, who, accompanied by a slave, decides to leave her husband and flee to Te Aea, near Matamata, pā of Tūpeteka, to seek refuge there.

Wairangi, however, realises that he is still fond of his senior wife, assembles a war party and sets off after her. On the way he finds discarded cloaks, and marks drawn on the rocks with red ochre, all signs left by Parewhete to indicate the route she has taken.

Eventually Parewhete is located at Te Aea, the pā of her relatives, who intend to murder Wairangi and his people to avenge the insult to her. Parewhete, however, warns Wairangi of the proposed plan and so he and his party have time to prepare for the inevitable battle. The signal to attack is a haka, te haka a Wairangi, which is still performed, particularly by the people of Ngāti Tūwharetoa. The warriors who lead the haka are Tama-te-hura, Ūpoko-iti, Pipito and finally, Wairangi. The Māori text reads as follows:

Ka tū a Tama-te-hura ka whakahua i te haka:

> Puhi kura, puhi kura, puhi kākā
> Ka whakatautapa ki Kāwhia
> Huakina, huakina.

Ka kī tērā hei tāna ka huaki. Ka noho ki raro. Kei runga ko Ūpoko-iti, ka whakahua i tāna haka:

> Ko Te Aea o ia rangi
> Ko Te Aea o ia rangi hui ake
> Ko Te Aea o ia rangi.

Ka kī hei tāna ka huaki. Ko Pipito, ka whakahua i tāna haka:

> Ka whakakōpura rua a Rangi-hape,
> Teina o Tūpeteka, e
> Huakina, huakina.

Ka tohe hei tāna ka huaki. Kātahi ka tū ko Wairangi ka whakahua:

> Tahi ka riri, toru ka whā
> E matamata hopukia
> Hōmai rā tō whiri kaha, toro kaha
> Kia wetewetea, wetewetea
> Ā tē, ā tā, ā tau.

Tama-te-hura rises and recites his haka:
> *The red top-knot, the kākā plume!*
> *Chant your challenge towards Kāwhia!*
> *Open, yes, thrust asunder!*

He says his haka should be the signal to attack. He sits down.
Then Ūpoko-iti rises and recites his haka:

It is Te Aea (the pā) of each day,
It is Te Aea (the pā) of each day,
Come together!
It is Te Aea (the pā) of each day
Of each day

He says at his haka they should attack. Then Pipito rises and
recites his haka:

Behold the lightning flash of Hape,
The younger brother of Tūpeteka,
Of Tūpeteka, of Tūpeteka!

He demands that the attack be made at his haka. Then Wairangi
rises and recites:

For it is war once more,
Seize your weapons!
Put forth your utmost strength
And sever the cords that bind you
Thus! and thus! and thus![3]

Wairangi is such a brilliant haka man that the audience is entranced by
him. As he begins his stanza his men reach for the patu concealed behind
their backs and they attack the people of Te Aea, with Tūpeteka being
Wairangi's first victim. Parewhete, by climbing onto the roof of the house,
escapes the slaughter and returns to Rurunui, near Wharepūhunga, located
to the west of Tokoroa, with Wairangi.

TAMA-RUA-RANGI AND TE RANGI-TŪ-MAI
Tama-rua-rangi of Te One pa, of Waimana, is lulled into a false sense
of security by the birdcalls of the enemy surrounding his pā. The
enemy realise that if they make too much noise the birds will fall silent
and rouse the suspicion of the garrison of the pā, so Maruiwi, chief of
the enemy, commands his men to imitate the sounds of certain birds.

Tama-rua-rangi, on hearing the bird calls, feels all is well but at day-
break Maruiwi attacks and Tama-rua-rangi's people are caught asleep
in the big communal sleeping house. As a consequence of the surprise
attack many of Tama-rua-rangi's people are killed but he, his son Te
Rangi-tū-mai, and a few others are captured, and taken to Rāroa pā,
Maruiwi's camp, on a bluff overlooking the Tauranga River, in the
Waimana Valley.

It is here that Maruiwi and his party prepare their hāngi for the feast,
and to ensure that Tama-rua-rangi will not escape they bind his limbs,
cover him with a cloak and fasten the edges of the cloak to stakes dri-
ven into the soil. The chief knows his time has come but tries to find a

way whereby his son, Te Rangi-tū-mai, might escape. So that his enemies will not realise his plan he remarks to his son:

E kī ana au i whāngaia koe ki te nene o te tāmure o Whangapānui, kia tiu koe, kia oha.

I say that you were fed on the uvula of the schnapper of Whangapānui that you might be active and strong to retain life.

The remark is incomprehensible to the enemy but the son realises that he is to make an attempt to escape. He asks his captors if he might have a taiaha as he would like to demonstrate his mastery of the weapon and to haka prior to his inevitable death. They give him the taiaha and surround him on three sides, the fourth being the bluff, which they consider too steep to descend and therefore not necessary to defend.

Te Rangi-tū-mai begins his performance and executes it so well that he is applauded. As he dances Te Rangi-tū-mai casts a glance in Tama-rua-rangi's direction and his father indicates that now is the time to make a bid for liberty. Te Rangi-tū-mai works his way towards the bluff then makes a jump for it, lands in the waters of the Tauranga below and escapes. At sunset Tama-rua-rangi is slain but his son lives on to seek revenge.

The ability to haka and to do so with style, grace, elegance and panache, was essential and extremely important in traditional Māori society. It is no less important in contemporary society. Throughout the Māori world individuals and groups, because of their reputations as performers of haka, enjoy a celebrity and status comparable to that of our forebears.

---

[1] Best, Elsdon. *Games and pastimes of the Māori.* p. 93. Wellington, Government Printer, 1976.

[2] Grey, Sir George. *Ngā mahi a ngā tūpuna.* Edited by H. W. Williams. 4th ed. Wellington, Reed, 1971.

[3] Biggs, Bruce; Hōhepa, P.; Mead, S. M. *Selected readings in Māori.* pp. 151-152. Wellington, Reed, 1967.

2

WHAT IS HAKA?

Ringa pākia
Uma tīraha
Turi whatia
Hope whai ake
Waewae takahia kia kino *

Slap the hands against the thighs
Puff out the chest
Bend the knees
Let the hip follow
Stamp the feet as hard as you can

When Hēnare Teōwai of Ngāti Porou, an acknowledged master of the haka, was on his deathbed he was asked by the late Wiremu Parker, broadcaster extraordinaire, 'What is the art of performing haka?' Hēnare Teōwai's reply was, 'Kia kōrero te katoa o te tinana' (The whole body should speak).

Kaitātaki:	Whakarongo rua aku taringa ki ngā kupu a te hunga mate e hākiri ake ana
Katoa:	Ko te haka he tohu whenua rangatira
	Ko te whakatinanatanga o ngā ihi o te rā
	I ngā wā o te raumati
	E tau ana ki runga i a Papa-tū-ā-nuku e takoto nei
Kaitātaki:	E ai ki ngā kupu kōrero, tokorua ngā wāhine a Tama-nui-te-rā
Katoa:	Auē! Ko Hine-raumati, ko Hine-takurua
	Ka puta ki waho ko tā Hine-raumati
	Ko Tāne-rore, ko Tāne-rore e
Kaitātaki:	He aha te koha mai a Tāne-rore ki te ao Māori?
Katoa:	Ko te haka, e ko te haka
	I puta ai te kōrero
	'E tū i te tū a Tāne-rore, e haka i te haka a Tāne-rore
	Kaua i te tū, i te haka a te keretao'
Kaitātaki:	Ko te taonga nui o te hakā?

---

* A haka from Te Arawa

In haka the whole body comes into play, particularly the face. The expression on the face can illustrate the meaning of the words quite graphically.

Katoa: Ko te whakaioio o te tinana
                     Ko te pūkana o te karu
                     Ko te whētero o te arero kia tāpapa tonu ki waho, hā!
                     Koinei rā hoki te ara
                     E puta ai ngā whakaaro o te hinengaro
                     Ā, hā! hā!

Kaitātaki: Ki ō tātou tīpuna, kāore he huna o te kupu e
Katoa: He tika rā! He tika rā!
                     I neherā, kāore he haka tātakimōri
                     Hou tonu atu ki ngā wāhi tapu o te tāne, o te wahine
                     Ngā kupu horetītī, ngā kupu nohunohu, e
                     Puritia te haka kia mau, kia ita
                     Ko te haka hoki he kupu kōrero
                     He mea whakairo e te ngākau
                     He mea whakapuaki e te māngai
                     He mea whakatū e te tinana
                     Auē, auē, auē taukuri e!

Leader: *I hearken to the words of my ancestors*
                     Resounding in my ears.
All: *The haka is a symbol of a noble land,*
                     It is the embodiment of the rays of the sun

In the days of summer,
Settling on Mother Earth lying beneath me.

Leader: *According to legend, Tama-nui-te-rā had two wives.*
All: *Aye! Hine-raumati and Hine-takurua*
And it was Hine-raumati
Who gave birth to Tāne-rore.

Leader: *What was Tāne-rore's gift to the world of the Māori?*
All: *The haka! Aye, the haka!*
Hence the saying,
'Adopt the stance of Tāne-rore
And haka as Tāne-rore does,
Do not adopt a puppet's stance
Nor perform as one!'

Leader: *What are the essential features of the haka?*
All: *That the body be virile and sinewy,*
The eyes be expressive,
And the tongue protrude full length,
For this is the avenue,
Whereby the thoughts of the mind are expressed.
Ā! hā! hā!

Leader: *Our elders were never afraid to say what they meant!*
All: *That is so true!*
In days gone by, no haka was meaningless,
No human activity sacrosanct,
Descriptions were explicit and graphic
Ā! hā! hā!
Therefore let us treasure the haka,
For the haka is a message,
Born of the soul,
Spoken by the mouth,
And expressed by the body
So be it![1]

Tama-nui-te-rā, the Sun God, had two wives, Hine-raumati, the Summer Maid, and Hine-takurua, the Winter Maid. The child born to him and Hine-raumati was Tāne-rore, who is credited with the origin of the dance. Tāne-rore is the trembling of the air as seen on the hot days of summer, and represented by the quivering of the hands in the dance.

Haka is the generic name for all Māori dance. Today, haka is defined as that part of the Māori dance repertoire where the men are to the fore with the women lending vocal support in the rear. Most haka seen today are haka taparahi, haka without weapons.

Vince Heperi

An essential feature of haka taparahi is that at some stage during the haka the performers sink to the ground. As the haka concludes, the performers rise once more to a standing position. Haka taparahi, traditionally, began and ended with the performers upright.

Haka, however, is more than dance. It is, as stated by the late Hāmana Mahuika of Ngāti Porou:

> . . . not merely a pastime, but it was also a custom of high social importance in the welcoming and entertainment of visitors. Tribal reputation often rose or fell on their ability to peform the haka.[2]

Of all the definitions of haka, that of Alan Armstrong in his book *Māori Games and Haka* (Reed, 1964), is the most apt and the most descriptive:

> The haka is a composition played by many instruments. Hands, feet, legs, body, voice, tongue and eyes all play their part in blending together to convey in their fullness the challenge, welcome, exultation, defiance or contempt of the words.
> It is disciplined, yet emotional. More than any other aspect of Māori culture, this complex dance is an expression of the passion, vigour and identity of the race. It is at its best, truly, a message of the soul expressed by words and posture . . .

---

[1] Kāretu, T. S. *Ngā waiata me ngā haka a te kapa haka o Te Whare Wānanga o Waikato.* pp. 22-22. Hamilton, University of Waikato, 1992.

[2] Dewes, Te Kapunga, ed. *Māori literature: He haka taparahi: men's ceremonial dance-poetry.* p. 2. Wellington, Department of Anthropology, Victoria University of Wellington, 1972.

3

EARLY OBSERVATIONS OF HAKA

Kaitātaki: Te mātātahi e,
E kīia mai nei
E kore te ao Māori e ora

Katoa: Engari mō tēnā!
Taku urupare, kupu paremata
Ki tēnei pōkahu, tēnei pāhewahewa
Kore, kore, kore rawa au e whakaae

Kaitātaki: Rere ana te whakapae
Nā te moe a Māori i a Pākehā
Kua kore haere te āhua Māori!

Katoa: Hei aha māku tēnā whakapae!
Ahakoa ōpure ōku karu,
Kehu ōku uru, tea tōku kiri
Me titiro kē ko taku ngākau,
Ko taku wairua
Kei reira kē e Māori ana
E kī ana hoki ahau,
'E kore au e hekeheke
He kākano rangatira.'

Kaitātaki: E noho nei ka kohuki a roto
He aha tēnei māherehere,
Tēnei mūkākā, tēnei pātaritari?

Katoa: Puta haere te ihu o Māori,
Kei tēnei tuku, kei tērā tuku
Tēnā karangatanga, kua tū he Māori
Tēnā karangatanga, kua tū he Māori
Nā tēnei, mānakanaka ana
Mānatunatu ana te ao Pākehā e

Kaitātaki: E ai ki te kōrero
Ko te nuinga o ngā Māori taiohi
Kei te hunga takahi ture
Kei te hunga koremahi

Katoa: Ki te tangohia te mana o te tangata
He aha kē ia te wāhi ki a ia?
He whāuruuru, he whakatumatuma!
Tōna whakatinanatanga he whānako,

He haurangi, he patu tangata
He aha kē rā i whakataruna ai
E pēnei nā te ao Māori?

Leader: *Young people, we are being told*
That the Māori will not survive.
All: *No way!*
My response, my retort
To this piece of misinformation and delusion
Is never, never, never will I agree!

Leader: *The contention is*
Because of intermarriage between Māori and Pākehā
The physical appearance of the Māori is in decline
All: *I take no cognisance ofsuch remarks!*
My eyes might be light in colour
My hair might be fair, my skin white
But look at my heart
And my soul
That is where I am Māori
And I state here,
'I will never be lost
For I am of the seed of chiefs.'

Leader: *I sit here and contemplate*
What are these words that arouse,
Stir and challenge the mind?
All: *The Māori is beginning to succeed*
In all walks of life
This profession, there are Māori
That profession, there are Māori
Consequently, there is apprehension
And anxiety in the Pākehā camp

Leader: *According to statistics*
The majority of the young Māori
Are among the law breakers
And the unemployed
All: *If you remove someone's self-respect*
What has he left?
He adopts a threatening posture, acts defiantly
Which manifests itself in theft,
Alcoholism and physical abuse
So why pretend to be surprised
At the behaviour of the young Māori?[1]

Ever since the first arrival of non-Māori in Aotearoa observations of haka have been recorded. It is fortunate that such has been the case for we are able to note how very little haka has changed in the interim despite the loudly voiced disapproval of early missionaries, the suppression of the language in the mainstream education system and the many distractions proffered by the world of the new arrivals.

. . . The dance *(haka)* then commenced amid the discharge of artillery. Each party formed an extended line of three ranks; the entire body of performers were mixed together, without reference to the rank they individually held in the community. The males were armed with muskets, which they brandished with much adroitness, so as to display the burnished stocks, on which much care had been expended. Those who were unable to procure this much-valued weapon, sported bayonets fixed to long spears, paddles, and even rail fencing *(taiapa)*. The females, single and married, widows and handmaids, added their efforts to this dance of welcome, but in order to give due effect and prepare for the exertion, they had stripped themselves to the waist, leaving their budding charms exposed to the gaze of their comrades, whose attention, be it said, was wholly confined to the dance. From the waist was appended a long garment of silken flax, that answered every purpose modesty could require, except when in the eagerness of the wearer's exertion, some treacherous belt betrayed the fidelity reposed in it, and let fall the only covering that otherwise answered every purpose, as long as it remained in the position assigned. In the chant that accompanies a dance, proper time was kept, as admirably tuned was the responsive chorus, whose effect must be heard to be appreciated, when issuing from the lips of a thousand performers, who at the same moment, to give increased effect to the sound, accompany the voice with a clap performed by the flattened right hand on the left breast, the whole body of performers apparently actuated by one well-timed impulse. The implements in their hands are instantly brandished, accompanied by shouts, yelling, howling, 'loud and loud', that threaten hard to destroy the auricular organs of the audience. At the same time their countenances are distorted into every possible shape the muscles of the human face can admit of, a leader giving a new grimace which is adopted instanter by all the performers, in the most exact union, rolling the eye-balls to and fro in their sockets, that at times the ball becomes almost inverted. This feat has the most diabolical appearance where a stain of blue pigment encircles the orbit of vision. The long tresses of hair worn by both sexes streaming loosely in the wind, and encircling countenances of a demoniacal cast, has an appearance that recalls to mind the Saxon traditions of our ancestors, or any army of Gorgons whose looks were reputed to change into stones those on whom they cast a glance, whose tresses were snakes, one of whom (Medusa) was placed by Perseus on the aegis of Minerva. The tongues of the performers were thrust out of their mouths, with an extension that rivalled the well-known chameleon, a feat accomplished by long habitual practice from early infancy. The whole effect gave an insight into the strong emotions these dances must produce in times of war, in raising the bravery of a party, and searing an antagonist, as also heightening the implacable hatred the belligerents must feel towards each other.[2]

It is inevitable that because pūkana (dilating of the eyes, performed by both sexes), whētero (the protruding of the tongue, performed by the men only), ngangahu (similar to pūkana, performed by both sexes), and pōtētē (the closing of the eyes at different points in the dance, performed by the women only), are essentials of Māori dance, that many observers confined themselves to such epithets as 'grotesque', 'savage', and 'indecent'.

Suddenly out dashed Rangiora, the enemy's chief, with huia feathers in his hair and a long spear in his hand, and, giving a yell of rage, he commenced to run up and down the ranks of his people, working himself and the tribe up to a pitch of frenzy. In perfect time, the warriors stamped the ground and beat their breasts, with their eyes hideously rolling and their tongues lolling out in derision. They looked like fiends from hell, wound up by machinery. The ground seemed to shake beneath their tread, and each time their hands struck their breasts there was a report like a hundred stock-whips being cracked at once.

And all this time the warrior chief danced up and down the ranks, chanting the war-song of his people, and every now and again the whole tribe would join in, as one man, with guttural yell of horrid hate.[3]

Not only Māori culture believes that the eyes are the windows of the soul and that the eyes can say much that the rest of the body cannot.

Pūkana, referred to by some of the early observers as 'rolling the eye-balls to and fro in their sockets' (J. S. Polack), is an essential feature of all Māori forms of dance. Both male and female pūkana but not all dancers are able to nor should all dancers. What is essential is that there be some dancers in the group who are able to do so and to do so with grace and style.

The Māori say, 'kia putē ngā karu,' dilate the eyes so that the whites are exaggerated and the pupils barely seen. This is pūkana. In the case of the female, the pūkana accompanied by a knowing smile can do

Vince Heperi

Karu pūkana!
Let the whites of the eyes be seen.
The eyes are the window to the soul and say much about the feelings of the
performer. If the eyes are inexpressive the performance is lack-lustre and
mediocre.

much to beguile and to allure. While the male does not smile in quite
the same way as the female, there is much that is attractive about the
male pūkana and whētero during the performance of the haka.

In the haka Tāne-rore[4], the question is posed: 'What are the essential
features of the haka?' Part of the response to that question is: '(That) the
eyes be expressive/ And the tongue protrude full length'.

Early observers noted that:

> . . . the tongues of the performers were thrust out of their mouths
> with an extension that rivalled the well-known chameleon, a feat
> accomplished by long habitual practice from early infancy . . . [5]

The haka Tāne-rore also refers to the fact that the tongue is the avenue
whereby the thoughts of the mind are conveyed to the audience. It is,
therefore, correct that the tongue should be so honoured as it is in carv-
ings of male ancestors, for it is the male who stands on the marae to
convey not only his personal thoughts but also the collective thoughts of
his people. Their mana rises, or falls, depending on his mastery of the
word. To be able to display that mastery the tongue is essential. Since
the female is not a principal speaker on the marae she does not whētero.

Within my own tribal area, Tūhoe, I have heard the following
philosophy expounded in seminars where elders debated issues of

30

tradition and culture at great length. The male has his penis to prove his manhood; it is an appendage that is visible. This, then, is the reason that the male extends his tongue full-length for it then becomes the symbol of his penis, of his manhood, during the dance. The female has no such visible appendage to prove her womanhood hence her not extending or protruding her tongue as the male does.

Every haka has a message, sometimes elementary, sometimes profound, but for that message to be conveyed the tongue is of the utmost importance. The tendency, today, for younger performers to protrude the tongue in a lizard-like way is to be deplored for it does not pay the tongue its just obeisance as is the case when the tongue is fully extended.

One does not whētero continuously throughout the haka for if one were to do so who would maintain the rhythm of the haka and ensure that its message is heard? Like pūkana, whētero is used to emphasise certain words, phrases or references in the haka. The use of the tongue as a means of defiance is a more recent philosophy subject to conjecture for, traditionally, the Māori had other ways of expressing defiance, the protruding of the tongue not being one of them.

Vince Heperi

Ko te arero kia tāpapa tonu ki waho.
Koinei rā hoki te ara
E puta ai ngā whakaaro o te hinengaro.
(The tongue should protrude full length
For this is the avenue
Whereby the thoughts of the mind are expressed.)

Museum of New Zealand

The role of manu ngangahu has been in decline in recent years. Such women can add much to the excitement of the haka, hence the need to encourage women to resume the role of manu ngangahu. In this photograph, taken at the Christchurch Exhibition in 1906-7, the manu ngangahu is positioned to the left.

The references to ' . . . distorting their countenances . . . ',[6] ' . . . this was a series of the most extravagant distortions of the features . . . ',[7] ' . . . their countenances are distorted into every shape the muscles of the human face can admit of . . . '[8] are all concerned with pūkana and whētero.

To the Māori mind the dance is mediocre or substandard if pūkana and whētero are absent. Other cultures need to appreciate from the outset that concepts of beauty vary and as one observer states ' . . . the dances of all savage nations are beautiful . . . '[9]

It is sad that the role of manu ngangahu, the women who perform to the side of the main troupe, has been in decline of late. A steady revival of this important female role in the haka has to be sustained and maintained but it is fortunate that some groups are beginning to revive the practice. It is the best pūkana women who assume the role of manu ngangahu.

I have seen a party of over one hundred men of Ngāti Tūwharetoa with only four women, two on either side of the party, their role being twofold: one, to protect the flank of the troupe, as these women are always armed; and two, to raise the flagging spirit of the troupe should such be necessary.

In haka, no area of human behaviour is sacrosanct. All is grist to the composer's mill. It might well have been such haka that caused early observers to note: ' . . . they frequently are such as to violate the laws of delicacy in point of gesture, grimace and other accompaniments . . . '[10] ' . . . they made use of the most indecent gestures . . . '[11] ' . . . but the gestures they make when singing are either very indecent or very grotesque . . . '[12] It needs to be borne in mind, however, that many of these early observers were refugees from Victorian Britain, so one ought not to be too surprised at their reactions.

The mind finds it difficult to accommodate the remarks of one observer: ' . . . They arose with their usual horrid scream . . . '[13] It is very difficult to 'scream' while performing haka and, in fact, no one 'screams' in haka. A more accurate observation is the following: ' . . . While their choked voices throbbed and sobbed or roared like those of tigers . . . '[14]

For haka to be exciting and enjoyable the leader must be able to keep good time and to inspire the troupe to give of their best, no half measures being acceptable. It is essential that the dancers be as follows: ' . . . The natives, like most other men in a state of nature, have no idea of half measures; thus, if they dance, they enter so much in the spirit of the amusement as to exhaust themselves by excessive fatigue . . . '[15] The reference, ' . . . they dance and caper about like mad monkeys . . . ',[16] a simile I do not consider to be apt, probably emanates from the movements of the haka and the ngangahu, the shrill high-pitched use of the voice during the haka. Frequently it is the women who perform this function for they are the manu ngangahu.

There were observers who appear to have had a serious interest in the haka and its social function, but there is still a prudish, if not prurient, obsession with the 'indecent' and 'immodest' in the context of haka. One could conclude that these adjectives emanate from a Christian and Victorian perspective. Haka run the whole gamut of human experience and those topics that one culture might find offensive or lewd are not so in another.

Many of the early anthropologists/ethnographers such as Elsdon Best, Percy Smith and Johannes Andersen, when confronted with a lyric considered, from their standpoint, to be indecent, would not translate it but would refer to the words as an 'effusion', or merely define the type of haka and give the lyric. It would seem that human behaviour is not for celebration in dance nor is its accompanying lyric to be translated!

The following comments indicate how well some early writers observed the haka:

On fine evenings, it is the favourite amusement of the young men and girls to assemble for the purpose of joining in this rude sort of concert. They may at these times be seen seated in a row, their hair dressed with feathers, and their faces smeared with red ochre and charcoal. The best voices commence and finish the verse. What may be called the refrain is shouted out by the united voices of the whole choir who, at the same time, form an accompaniment by slapping one hand on the breast, while the other hand is raised aloft and made to vibrate, so as to produce on the eye an effect analogous to that of the shake in music. This vibrating of the hand is called kakapa . . . Each verse of the haka is a separate sentence,

Augustus Earle (1793-1838) was one of the earliest visitors to record his impressions of the haka. This engraving 'A dance of New Zealanders' is from his A narrative of a nine months' residence in New Zealand in 1827.

complete in itself, terminated by what I have called the refrain, which is a peculiar guttural noise, caused by repeated inspirations, succeeded by forcible expirations of the breath. When there are many singers the effect is strange, and not unpleasing; but the performance is frequently accompanied by gestures of the body of an immodest character . . . [17]

In some instances one might consider the words of praise and admiration to be a little too excessive and extravagant:

The dances of all savage nations are beautiful, but those of the New Zealanders partake also of the horrible. The regularity of their movements is truly astonishing; and the song, which always accompanies a dance, is most harmonious. They soon work themselves up to a pitch of frenzy; the distortions of their face and body are truly dreadful, and fill the mind with horror. Love and war are the subjects of their songs and dances; but the details of the latter passion are by far the most popular among them. I was astonished to find that their women mixed in the dance indiscriminately with the men, and went through all those horrid gestures with seemingly as much pleasure as the warriors themselves . . . [18]

Haka has always been a spectacle enjoyed or abhorred by those who have seen it being performed. It is, however, unfortunate that many of

South Australian Museum

War Dance by George French Angas from The New Zealanders *(1846). The haka was frequently performed naked, as in this representation of a group which has just landed by canoe at Ohinemutu, Rotorua.*

those enjoying the performance do not understand what is being said but are rather reacting to the excitement that good performers can engender in their audiences. No reaction indicates a mediocre performance.

Many tribes began to perform haka less and less as the influence of the missionaries became stronger. So much so that one tribe from one area had to teach another so that it could properly assume its role as host at the 1934 Waitangi celebrations. Fortunately, the majority of the tribes refused to let the missionaries dictate to them so haka continued to thrive.

[1] Kāretu,Timoti. S. *Ngā waiata me ngā haka a te kapa haka o Te Whare Wānanga o Waikato.* pp. 31-34. Hamilton, University of Waikato, 1992.

[2] Polack, Joel Samuel. *Manners and customs of the New Zealanders.* V.1 pp. 86-88. Christchurch, Capper, 1976. Facsimile of edition published London, Madden, 1840.

[3] Browne, C. R. *Māori witchery: native life in New Zealand.* p. 61. London, Dent, 1929.

[4] Kāretu, Timoti S. *op.cit.* pp. 21-22.

[5] Polack, J. S. *op. cit.* p. 88.

[6] Marsden, Samuel. *Letters and journals of Samuel Marsden, 1765-1838.* p. 502. Edited

by J. R. Elder. Dunedin, Coulls, Somerville Wilkie and A. H. Reed for the Otago University Council, 1932.

[7] Barthorp, Michael. *To face the daring Māoris.* p. 141. London, Hodder and Stoughton, 1979.

[8] Polack, J. S. *op. cit.* p. 88.

[9] Earle, Augustus. *A narrative of a nine months' residence in New Zealand in 1827.* p.62. Christchurch, Whitcombe & Tombs, 1909.

[10] Savage, John. *Some account of New Zealand, particularly the Bay of Islands and surrounding country, with a description of the religion and government, language, arts, manufactures, manners and customs of the natives, & c.& c.* p. 85. London, J. Murray & A. Constable, 1807; Christchurch, Capper Press, 1973.

[11] McNab, Robert. *Historical Records of New Zealand,* Vol.2, p. 283. Wellington, Government Printer, 1914.

[12] Ibid., p. 335.

[13] Marsden, Samuel. *op. cit.* p. 502.

[14] Sharp, Andrew, ed. *Duperrey's visit to New Zealand in 1824.* p. 48. Wellington, Alexander Turnbull Library, 1971.

[15] Savage, John. *op.cit.* p. 85.

[16] Maning, F. E. *Old New Zealand.* p. 44. Christchurch, Whitcombe & Tombs, 1956.

[17] Shortland, Edward. *Traditions and superstitions of the New Zealanders.* 2nd ed. London, Longman, Brown, Green, Longmans & Roberts, 1856.

[18] Earle, Augustus. *op.cit.* pp. 62-63.

4

TYPES OF HAKA

The repertoire of haka comprises, in the main, haka taparahi, where the performers line up in serried ranks and perform set actions. Tāne-rore is a haka taparahi, defined by the late Arapeta Marukitipua Awatere, an acknowledged master of the haka, in *The Journal of the Polynesian Society*, Vol. 84, No. 4, December, 1975: 'From pre-European days to the present a haka taparahi has always been a ceremonial, never a war dance, always performed without weapons.'

PERUPERU

Erroneously defined by generations of uninformed as 'war dances', the true 'war dance' is the whakatū waewae, the tūtū ngārahu and the peru-peru, defined by Awatere as follows:

> The peruperu is the true war-dance and is performed with weapons when the warriors come face to face with the enemy in battle. Because it is the true war-dance, its purpose ought to be explained. Hard conditioning makes the warriors physically and mentally fit to perform this dance which has the psychological purpose of demoralising the enemy by gestures, by posture, by controlled chanting, by conditioning to look ugly, furious to roll the fiery eye, to glare the light of battle therein, to spew the defiant tongue to control, to distort, to snort, to fart the thunder of the war-god upon the enemy, to stamp furiously, to yell raucous, hideous, blood-curdling sounds, to carry the anger, the peru, of Tuumatauenga, the ugly-faced war-god, throughout the heat of battle. Peruperu is the intensive form of peru 'anger' and this is how the war-dance got its name, and that is its psychological purpose which no other form of haka could match in the past, can match now nor ever will. The peruperu ever took pride of place in the warrior-armour of the tamataane of yore . . .

The outstanding feature of the peruperu is the high leap off the ground with the legs folded under.

Uhi, uhi mai te waero

Aha, toutoua, auē.
Uhi, uhi mai te waero,
E ko roto ko taku puta

Koia anō he peruperu! (It is indeed the peruperu!)
Ngāti Tuwharetoa perform the peruperu at the ceremony acknowledging the gift of
land at Waitangi to the nation by Lord Bledisloe, 6 February 1934. An essential
feature of the peruperu is that all the performers be armed and the legs should be
tucked under (peruperu) each time they leap into the air.

He puta aha te puta?
He puta tohu te puta,
E rua nei ko te puta,
Hei!

Koia anō, koia anō!
Koia anō he peruperu.
Inā hoki te taiaroa,
I whakatirohia mai nei ki te whanga.
Ahā! Pare rewha, pare rewha!
Pare rewha

Leader:	Kumekumea!
All:	Tōtoia!
Leader:	Kumekumea!
All:	Tōtoia!

Ā e tō rā ki te tahataha,
Ā e tō rā ki te taparere,
Ngā kōkako huataratara
Ki Waikurekure hā!
Ā ki Waikurekure, hā!
Ā ki Waikurekure, hā!

Gird yourself in the dogskin cloak,

And leap into the fray!
The battle, what of it?
Warrior meets warrior man to man,
Ha! the battle is joined.

It is indeed!
It is indeed!
The war dance!
Here is the good sign and omen
Viewed from afar.
Aha! The lifting eyebrows give their assent!

Draw it hither! Drag it thither!
Draw it hither! Drag it thither!
Draw it to the edge of the cliff,
Drag it to the brink of the precipice!
The serrated plumes of the chequered kōkako.
Ah, to Waikurekure!
Ah, to Waikurekure![1]

Tūtū Ngārahu

To some people the terms peruperu, whakatū waewae and tūtū ngārahu are synonymous. However, each type has its own peculiarity.

Like the peruperu, the men who perform tūtū ngārahu are armed. Unlike the peruperu, the jumping is not up and down but rather from side to side as seen in the formal rituals of welcome performed by the tribes of the north.

The following is a tūtū ngārahu from the tribes of the north:

Ka Eke I Te Wīwī

Ka eke i te wīwī
Ka eke i te wāwā
Ka eke i te pāparahua
I Rangitumu,
Huia! Ka eke!

The outer palisade is breached
The second palisade is breached
The innermost palisade is breached
At Rangitumu
Assemble! Victory is ours![2]

Whakatū Waewae

This is a haka in which the men are armed but, unlike the peruperu, there is no jumping.

Te Puru

Kaea:	Ringa i poua!
	Ko te puru! E ko te puru koa!
Katoa:	Whakatangatanga ki runga!
	Whakatangatanga ki raro!
	E kore te ora e tae mai ki konei,
	I te ture o te mate!
	Pūkawautia koa!
	Aha tē! Aha tā! Aha te riri e!
Kaea:	Aha ko ngā ngirangira, ko ngā hotahota,
	O te whītau, tapahia!
Katoa:	Ka! E! Hō!
Kaea:	Ka awheawhea te rua tamariki!
Katoa:	Ka! E! Hō!
Kaea:	Nāu anō i whai mai ki aku nui!
Katoa:	Ka! E! Hō!
Kaea:	I kite ai koe!
Katoa:	Ka! E! Hō!
Kaea:	I taku tou rape!
Katoa:	Ka! E! Hō!
	I te rā nui o te tara
	O te whītau, tapahia!
	Ka! E! Hō!
	Hei!

Begin with a striking action up and down!
It is a war party!
But a war party of joy!
All together we thrust up!
All together we thrust down!
We cannot be harmed except in battle
Because we are immune to evil!
So bind yourself together!
And into the fray!
Cut away the useless parts,
The immature people, the untested ones!
Our work cannot be done by the young!
Respond to the commands and actions, and
Follow me to my heights!
For all is now in readiness![3]

In the case of Tūhoe, when the men have completed the whakatū waewae they retire to permit the women to emerge with greenery in their

hands to perform their part of the ceremony. Once the women have concluded their performance they retire and together with the men, who are now again to the fore, perform a haka taparahi.

The fact that the matua, the welcoming party, is now unarmed indicates to the guests that it is accepted that they come with peaceful intent.

NGERI

Ngeri are short haka 'to stiffen the sinews, to summon up the blood', but, unlike haka taparahi, have no set movements, thereby giving the performers free rein to express themselves as they deem appropriate. Most of the best-known haka of the Māori repertoire are, in fact, ngeri, which are performed, in most instances, without weapons.

He Oranga Mai

He oranga mai hoki tātou
I te parekura i Manawa-toki-tū
Tū ko te hika o tō whāea
Kia matapopore mai ki te pirau o tō whanaunga
Whanaunga mate ki te pō, tini o te pō, mano o te pō
Ā! hā! ngā korekore o te pō
Ā! hei te pō, hei te pō
Hei te ao, hei te ao
Ā! hei te pō, hei te pō
Hei te ao, hei te ao,
Ka whero e
Ka whero e
Ka whero koia te ngutu o taua wahine, o taua tangata
Whakapua kōwhai, ngutu-kākā, pārera tokitoki
I!
Mā wawai e momia te tai o te kōwhewhe tūtata
Ka haere tēnei ki te tiki tārewarewa
Mō ana moko hei aha?
Hei whakakote tamutamu
Nō whea atu ko te tamutamu?
Nō Te Aopuhi kē ko te tamutamu!
Kī mai nei Rehua-hia māna anake te kōkihi
Au, auē mate
Ki mai nei Rehua-toro māna anake te kororā
Au, auē mate te kororā
Kūkutia! Wherawherahia!
Ki te tohe mai ia he aha te kai mā te niho kehokeho
He keho anō!
Tū ana te kehokeho!
Ngaua ki ō niho, he mamae poto
Kei pakoko kei tua tērā whaitua

41

Tihē!

We are the survivors
Of the massacre at Manawa-toki-tū
There, where the body of your mother was violated
Be aware of the putrefaction of your kin
Your kin who have been lost to the world of night
to the many in the world of night
At night
and during the day
They are red
They are red.
Red indeed are the lips of that man/woman and woman/man
Red as the kākā beak kōwhai and the bill of the brown duck
I!
Who will suck out the pus of the boil about to burst?
He goes to fetch the tārewarewa for his descendants
For what purpose?
To make them suck vulva?
Whose vulva is it?
It is the vulva of Te Aopuhi!
Rehua-hia says that the kōkihi is for him alone
Hence the destruction of the kōkihi
Rehua-toro says that the penguins are for him alone
Hence the destruction of the penguin
So hold tight, then open wide
Should he persist in asking what the food for the vulva's teeth is
Tell him it is vulva!
Long live the vulva!
Sink in your teeth! The pain is short!
Lest that region wither
So let there be life![4]

Manawa Wera

Manawa wera and pōkeka, similar in style to ngeri, do not have set movements.

In Tūhoe, manawa wera were performed at funerals, unveilings, or hari mate, ceremonies connected with the dead. Today, they are still performed on such occasions but are beginning to be used on other occasions as well.

Taka Mai I Hea?

Taka mai i hea te pō o te rangi?
Taka mai i runga o ngā maunga e
Takoto koutou ki runga ki ngā marae tapu

42

Ki te Ika Nui, ki Te Ika Roa, ki Te Ika-a-Māui-tikitiki-o-Taranga
E takoto nei
Haere rā, e koro, mana o ngā tīpuna
Te puhi o Tūhoe
Ka taupoki te waka ki raro rā
E, ka taupoki

From whence comes the darkening of the heavens?
It comes from the mountain tops
Rest in peace on the sacred marae of the Big Fish, the Long Fish
The Fish of Māui-tikitiki-o-Taranga,
Lying here
Farewell, sir, the pride of our ancestors
The nobility of Tūhoe
The canoe is overturned
Indeed overturned.[5]

PŌKEKA

Pōkeka, a term peculiar to the tribes of Te Arawa, are like manawa wera except that there is no specific occasion on which' they are deemed to be more appropriate than any other.

He Aha Rā Kei Te Tau o Taku Ate?

Kaea:	He aha rā kei te tau o taku ate
	E haehae ake nei?
Katoa:	Ko te mamae ki te ngaro o taku reo!
	Warea kē ana ngā whakahaere Māori o te motu
	Me te iwi whānui hoki
	Ki te reo o tauiwi!
	E kore e ora i ngā kōhanga reo,
	Te Ātaarangi, ngā kura reorua, ngā whare wānanga
	Eaoia mā te kōrero tonu! Mā te kōrero tonu!
	E tātou, e te ao Māori, e tau nei
	Kāti rā te toupiore, te māikoiko
	Kei riro kē mā te Pākehā tō tātou reo e pupuri.
	Takatū ake! Takatū ake!
	Takatū ake kia whai kiko ai te kōrero,
	'Tōku reo, tōku ohooho,
	Tōku reo, tōku māpihi maurea,
	Tōku reo, tōku whakakai marihi.'
	Auē! Auē! Auē! Te mamae ki taku taonga e!
	Hei!

What is this tearing me apart?
It is the pain at the loss of my language.

43

To perform haka with élan and panache one must give one's all — there are no half measures. If one is still able to speak after a performance, one has not given one's all.

*Māori organisations throughout the country
And the Māori people themselves
Prefer the language of the Pākehā,
How can ours survive if that situation persists?
It will not survive because of kōhanga reo,
Te Ātaarangi, bilingual schools or universities
But by being spoken all the time.
We, the Māori, here assembled
Be dilatory and indigent no longer
Lest it be left to the Pākehā to keep our language alive
Do not permit this situation to occur
Let us act together so that these words are meaningful,
'My language, my cherished possession
My language, my object of affection
My language, my precious adornment.'
Auē! Auē! Auē! What pain I feel at the loss of
   something so valuable![6]*

HAKA PŌWHIRI

Haka pōwhiri, haka of welcome, as performed by the women of Ngāti Porou and Te Whānau-a-Apanui appear to have no counterpart elsewhere.

On the more formal occasions the tribes of the eastern seaboard, in particular Ngāti Porou, welcome their guests with the women to the fore performing haka pōwhiri. It is not until the women have performed their part of the ceremony that the men emerge to conclude the rituals of welcome with a haka taparahi. Ngāti Porou, on the occasion of formal welcomes to important guests, is probably one of the few tribal areas where the men are not to the fore initially.

Te Urunga Tū, Te Urunga Pae

Kaea:	Tēnā i whiua! Taku pōhiri e rere atu rā Ki te hiku o te ika, Te puku o te whenua, Te pane o te motu, Ki te whakawhititanga i Raukawa Ki te Waipounamu, e . . .
Katoa:	E, i aha tērā! E, haramai koe i te pōhiritanga A taku manu Haramai koe i te pōhiritanga A taku manu!
Kaea:	He tīwaiwaka ahau nā Māui
Katoa:	Tiori rau e hē hā!
Kaea:	He tīwaiwaka ahau nā Māui
Katoa:	Tiori rau e hē hā!
Kaea:	Te urunga tū, te urunga pae
Katoa:	Te urunga mātiketike!
Kaea:	Te urunga tū, te urunga pae
Katoa:	Te urunga mātiketike!
Kaea:	Ko tōu aro i tahuri mai Ko tōku aro i tahuri atu
Katoa:	Tākina ko au, tākina ko koe!
Kaeā	Ko tōu aro i tahuri mai Ko tōku aro i tahuri atu
Katoa:	Tākina ko au, tākina ko koe
Kaea:	Porou koa!
Katoa:	Ko Hamo te wahine koa!
Kaea:	Ko Tahu koa!
Katoa:	Ko Hamo te wahine koa Nāna i tohatoha ki Nui Tīreni

Women of Ngāti Porou performing the haka pōwhiri, 'Te Urunga Tū', on the occasion of the centenary of Porourangi Meeting House celebrated in 1990.

Vince Heperi

Ka hīpoki!
Haere mai! Haere mai!
Haere mai! Haere mai!
Ki taku hui! Hei!

Solo:	*Begin with a swing!*
	My call has gone forth
	To the tail of the fish
	To the belly of the land
	To the head of the island
	And across the Straits of Raukawa
	To the South Island
All:	*The invitation has gone forth!*
	So come you at the welcome
	Call of my bird
	Respond to the cry
	Of my bird's welcome!
Solo:	*I am a fantail of Māui*
All:	*Chirping restlessly to and fro!*
Solo:	*I am a fantail of Māui*
All:	*Singing and darting here and there!*
Solo:	*The vertical entering*
	The horizontal entering!
All:	*The entering erect!*
Solo:	*You turn to me*
	And I will turn to you
All:	*I challenge and you challenge!*

Solo:	You respond to me
	And I respond to you
All:	I challenge and you challenge!
Solo:	It is Porou indeed!
All:	And Hamo his wife too!
Solo:	It is Tahu indeed!
All:	And Hamo was his wife also!
	Their progeny are found throughout New Zealand!
	So welcome to you!
	Welcome to my gathering![7]

KAIORAORA

Kaioraora are vehicles expressly for the venting of hatred. Every tribe has composed them and every tribe has been the inspiration for their composition. Kaioraora literally means to eat alive. Such is the anger and hatred of the composer that she (in most instances the composers of this genre of haka are women) would like to eat alive the perpetrators of the dastardly deed that prompted the anger and the hatred.

To be the reason, the inspiration, for the composition of a haka was, and still is, considered a signal honour no matter how virulent the hatred expressed in the lyric.

Today, many of the kaioraora are preserved and retained by the tribe who are the butt of the composition rather than the tribe who composed it.

The following kaioraora was composed by Hine-i-tūrama, a composer of renown from Te Arawa, to express her hatred and disgust for Tūhoe for having killed her husband and not permitting her to take his corpse back with her so that she might mourn him in the customary way. She was permitted to take his head but the body was retained.

E hiakai atu ana ahau ki Ruatāhuna, ki Kaimokopuna
Ki te okiokinga o te ūpokokohua nei, o Te Urewera
He kore e nuia te hau kana
Nāna anō i rere tawheta noa ki te riri
Ki te kawe nui atu mō Tūhoe, mō Tū-mata-whero
Kia whakarauikatia te pōkai kōtuku nā Rangitihi
He paenga pakake ki te ao o te tonga
Kia tātaia ki runga ki te turuturu poto
Kia titiro iho ki te hoa o te kai, ki a Tāwhaki
Ki te kiri rā i whakataua ki te anuhe tawatawa.

How I long to sink my teeth into Ruatāhuna and Kaimokopuna
Dwelling place of these bastards, Te Urewera
No heed was taken of the portents
And so, recklessly, they went to war

47

To battle it out with Tūhoe and Tū-mata-whero
Now, lying together are the high born of Rangitihi
Like stranded whales in the South
Oh that from the short poles on which they are displayed
They might gaze down on the ceremonial feast of Tāwhaki
Upon the skin likened to that of the mottled mackerel.[8]

These then are the types of haka still performed today.

---

[1] Believed to be of Ngāti Tūwharetoa origin.

[2] Kāretu, Timoti S. *Ngā waiata me ngā haka a tāua, a te Māori.* p. 70. Hamilton, University of Waikato, 1978.

[3] Kāretu, Timoti S. *Ngā waiata me ngā haka a te kapa haka o Te Whare Wānanga o Waikato.* pp. 1-4. Hamilton, University of Waikato.

[4] *Ibid.* pp. 11-12.

[5] From a collection of Tūhoe haka and chants held by the author.

[6] Kāretu, Timoti S. *op. cit.* pp. 75-76.

[7] *Reception to Her Majesty the Queen, His Royal Highness the Duke of Edinburgh, His Royal Highness the Prince Charles and Her Royal Highness the Princess Anne by the Māori people.* Gisborne, 22 March, 1970. pp. 2-3. Wellington, Government Printer, 1970.

[8] From a collection of Tūhoe haka and chants held by the author.

5

THEMES OF HAKA

Haka have always reflected the cares, concerns and issues of the time. The haka of today are no different, as illustrated by this composition of Ngāpō Wehi, tutor and mentor of Wakahuia, one of the most outstanding groups in Aotearoa today. At the 1992 Aotearoa Māori Performing Arts Festival, this was the winning haka. The translation is that of the composer:

Kaitātaki:	Ko koe tonu rā tōu nā kaipatu e!
	Ko koe tonu rā tōu nā kaipatu e!
	Nō mua o te taenga mai o tauiwi mā
	Inā te pakari o te tinana Māori e.
Katoa:	Me pakari rā ka tika, nā te mea ko wāna kai hoki rā
	He kūmara, he pikopiko, he aruhe, he hua rākau, he ika,
	He manu me ngā kai moana katoa e.
Kaitātaki:	Nō te taenga mai rā o tauiwi mā
	Ka mauria mai rā ētahi kai tino kino e
Katoa:	Ko aua kai rā, he tote, he huka, paura parāoa,
	Waipiro me te nanakia tupeka e
Kaitātaki:	Nō te huritanga mai rā o tēnei rau tau,
	Kua kitea, kei te kitea ngā hua
Katoa:	Mate huka, mate manawa, mate ia toto, mate huangō,
	Mate pupuhi tinana me ngā momo mate pukupuku katoa e
Kaitātakī	Ko koe tonu rā tōu nā kaipatu e!
Katoa:	E kore rawa te kai, te paipa me te waipiro e uru ki tō waha
	Mehemea kāore nāu i puru atu ki roto
Kaitātaki:	Ko koe tonu rā tōu nā kaipatu e!
Katoa:	E umere nei ngā iwi mō ngā aituā tūtuki waka
	Nā te waipiro hoki rā tāna mahi
Kaitātaki:	Ahakoa i tērā tau e ono rau tāngata i riro i runga i ngā rori
Katoa:	E kore rawa rā e tata atu ki te whā mano tāngata ka mate
	I te kai paipa e, tēnei kai kōhuru, tēnei mate kurī
	E patu nei i te tinana i te wā e ora tonu ana
Kaitātaki:	E kī nei te kōrero, me aro ki te hā o Hine-ahu-one
Katoa:	Whakarongo mai rā, wāhine mā!

Dr A. S. Thomson (1817-1860) gave this vivid impression of 'The War Dance' in The Story of New Zealand *(1857), the first major history of the country. Notice the use of muskets in the haka rather than traditional weaponry.*

Ko koutou kē kei mua o te ao mō te kai paipa e
Me pēhea rā e pakari tonu ai te tinana
Ki te tohetohe tonu koe ki te kai i taua kai

Kaitātaki:	Ko koe tonu rā tōu nā kaipatu e!
Katoa:	Kei a koe rā te whare tangata
	Kaua e takakinotia, whāngaia rā tō tamaiti
	Ki ngā kai tōtika, kia hoki ai ki te wā o mua
	O te taenga mai o tauiwi mā

KO KOE TONU RĀ TŌU NĀ KAIPATU E!

You are your own destroyer! You are your own exterminator!

Prior to the arrival of the foreigner, the Māori was a beautifully developed physical specimen. Indeed he was because he ate a well-balanced diet: starch provided by his Gods, fern fronds (greens), fern roots, fruit and berries, fish, poultry, plus all the many varieties of seafoods available.

When the foreigner arrived, he brought with him some body-destroying foods such as salt, sugar, flour, booze and the rogue or scoundrel – tobacco! By the turn of this century, we will have seen and will probably continue to see the outcomes of such foods like diabetes, heart disease, high blood pressure, asthma, gout, obesity, plus the many forms of cancers.

You are your own killer! No way can food, tobacco or booze enter

your mouth by accident because YOU alone and no one else is respon-
sible for putting them there. You can actually be your own saviour.

We become very emotive about the number of road deaths each
year, many of which relate to drinking. Although last year, 600-
odd road fatalities were recorded, these figures do not compare
to the 4,000-odd smoke-related deaths each year (of which 600
are Māori) – a meaningless waste of life. This murderous habit
slowly but surely kills the body whilst still living.

It is said that we should take heed of the woman's voice, well lis-
ten here ladies – YOU lead the world in the field of smoking!
Explain to me how we can produce healthy bodies if you persist
in continuing to inhale that stuff! You are the destroyer because
you are the repository of mankind.

Don't abuse or defile your body. Rather, feed your child with the
very best of foods so that we may go back to the time prior to the
arrival of the foreigner.

Think about it, you could actually be your own monitor or saviour
of your children, grandchildren, and future generations.

All tribes have haka peculiar to them which are not often heard outside
of their own tribal boundaries. Such haka as Rūaumoko, Kura Tīwaka
and Poropeihana, originating from Ngāti Porou on the east coast of
Aotearoa, are considered by some people to be the classics of the haka
repertoire. Certainly, during and after World War II the influence of
Ngāti Porou in haka and waiata-ā-ringa was strong, as their compositions in both fields were the most popular.

In the main, it has been the male Māori boarding schools that have
ensured the continued performance of such haka as Rūaumoko, Kura
Tīwaka and Poropeihana. While many of the allusions and references in
these haka are unknown to the younger performers, the haka still enjoy
great popularity. Ngāti Porou still perform these haka, with Rūaumoko
being the one that is performed on the most formal of occasions.

One of the very positive outcomes of the Māori Performing Arts
Festival is that many haka have been composed with widely diverging
themes. The following are some of these haka.

The majority of the Māori population are young, 39 per cent being
under fifteen years of age as at the 1986 census. This younger compo-
nent of the Māori population wish to be heard and to be considered in
the decisions which impinge on their futures.

Kaitātaki:	E koutou, e ngā kaihautū o te waka o te iwi Māori!
Katoa:	Taringa whakarongo e!
	Aroha mai rā ki ahau, ki te rangatahi e ngunguru nei
	E whiua nei ki te kōrero

He tamariki takahi tikanga, he tamariki wāwāhi tahā
Engari nā koutou anō hoki te kōrero
He tangi tō te tamariki, he whakamā tō ngā mātua
Auē! Auē! Auē! Taukuri e!

Kaitātaki: Kei pōhēhē mai koutou, e aku kaumātua
Kei te whakawātia koutou e
Katoa: Korekore rawa! Korekore rawa!
Nā te uaratanga kē o te ngākau
I rere tawheta noa ai te kupu
I takahi ai au nā te kūare e

Kaitātaki: E koro mā, e kui mā, anei taku tono e!
Katoa: Huakina mai te tatau o tō whare
Kia kite au i ngā taonga whakahirahira a ōku tīpuna
Kia whītiki ake au i taku hope ki te maurea whiritoi
Kia uhi au i ahau ki taku kākahu kura
He tikitiki ki tōku rae
Kia mōhio ai au ki taku taha rangatira e

Kaitātaki: Ahakoa mātou nō Te Whare Wānanga o Waikato
He whare wānanga Pākehā kē
Katoa: Auē! He tika rā! He tika rā!
Kei konei kē te mana, te ihi, te wehi, te tapu
Kei aku tīpuna marae, kei aku tīpuna whare
Kei aku maunga kōhātanga, kei aku wai tipua
Kia kī ake ahau, ahakoa pēhea
E kore au e ngaro, te kākano i ruia mai i Rangiātea

Leader: *You, the leaders of the Māori people*
All: *Lend us your ears!*
Have some sympathy for us, the younger generation
making itself heard
Who are being criticised as follows
Young people who walk over custom, who have no
consideration for others
But remember it was you who said
If children cry, it is the parents who feel the shame

Leader: *You, my elders, might think that I stand here in*
judgement of you
All: *Such is not the case!*
It is because of the strong desire within me
That I say things without thinking
The reason I offend is because I know no better

Leader: *O my elders, here is my request*

Sir Apirana Ngata leads the haka at the opening of the meeting house at Waitangi in 1940. Ngata inspired a revival in Maori culture during the first half of the twentieth century, and encouraged haka competition.

All:	*Open up the doors of your house*
	That I might see the stately treasures bequeathed by
	my ancestors
	Let me gird my waist with the maurea whiritoi
	Enshroud myself in my cloak of bright plumage
	And on my brow a tīpare
	So that I will appreciate my noble origins
Leader:	*Though we are students of the University of Waikato*
	It is a Pākehā institution!
All:	*That is indeed true!*
	My source of prestige, of pride, of awe, and of
	sacredness is here
	On my ancestral marae, in my ancestral house
	In my echoing mountains and in my sacred rivers
	So I can say that no matter what happens
	I will never be lost for I am of the seed sown at
	Rangiātea![1]

Solutions are sought to problems resulting from the majority culture's dominance and so the question is posed:

Kaitātaki: E tātou, e te ao Māori, kei hea rā te rongoā?

53

Katoa: Kei a tātou tonu! Kei a tātou tonu!
           Kaua tātou e tukua kia rite ki te keretao
           Hūtia te aho, peke pēnei, peke pērā!
           Huri mai tātou ki te ao o ngā tīpuna
           Ki ōna whakaaro tiketike, whakaaro hōhonu
           Kia whakataukī ake i konei
           Hei whakarongo mai mā te ao Pākehā
           He whetū ka haere ki te kai i te marama:
           Kei te taha ki tōna hoa riri
           E kore rā ia e toa
           Anā! Anā! Anā tō kai e! Hei!

Leader: *We, the Māori, where does the solution lie?*
All: *Within ourselves! Within ourselves!*
           Let us no longer be manipulated like puppets
           Who, when the string is pulled, jump this way and that
           Rather, let us return to the world of our forebears
           To its noble and profound philosophies
           So that we can state quite categorically
           For the Pākehā to hear
           A star sets off to devour the moon
           As far as his enemy is concerned
           He, the star, will never succeed!
           So! Let that sum up my feelings! Hei![2]

However, despite the problems of contemporary life, many of the
young have a strong feeling for, and an active interest in, tradition and
custom. Their concerns are expressed in this haka:

Kaitātaki: Hānuere te marama
            Tahi mano, waru rau, waru tekau mā rua te tau
            Puta i a Te Tūruki ana kupu whakaari
            Ki a Ngāti Awa mō tōna whare, mō Rua-taupare
Katoa: Āe, ka pai hoki tō koutou whare
            Oti anō, te raruraru e titiro ake nei ahau
            Kei te whawhai tētahi o ngā pakitara
            Ki tētahi o ngā pakitara
            Te whatitoka ki te tūārongo
            Te taina ki te tuakana
            Te tamaiti ki te matua

Kaitātaki: Rau tau kua pahure
            Pēhea ngā kupu a Te Tūruki?
Katoa: Hāngai pū tonu! Hāngai pū tonu!
            Tahuri te tamaiti ki tōna matua
            Te taina ki tōna tuakana

Tūpehupehuhia, tūkarikarihia
Te kupu a ngā heinga
Mā te tuakana ka tōtika te taina
Tōna tikanga rā hoki
He taunaki, he tautāwhi
Ehara kē i te takatakahi a tētahi
I te mana o tētahi

Kaitātaki:	He aha kē ia tā te tamaiti?
Katoa:	Noho puku! Mātai! Whakaoko!

Mate rawa te matua
Tāngutungutu, pūioio, pāuaua
Kore rawa e ekea e te kōrero
Kāore e tae te waewae kai pakiaka
Ki te waewae kai kapua
Arā kē ia
Tamaiti i ākona ki te kāinga
Tūnga ki te marae, tau ana

Kaitātaki:	Tēnei ahunga e pōhau nei
	I te tauira hei tūrukitanga
	Ka kite kē i ngā huihuinga-ā-iwi
Katoa:	Tū te matua, tū te tamaiti

Tū te tuakana, tū te taina
Poautinitini, tū te whare mate
Tā nehe whakatau
Kai pirau! Kai pirau!

Kaitātaki:	Kāti! Kei hea rā he huringa ake
	Mō te mātātahi?
Katoa:	Tōna tikanga kei ngā marae, kei ngā pakeke

Engari koia tonu rā ngā wāhi
E takahia nei ngā tohutohu
Āe, ko ngā kai o te whare
He kōhatu, he kirikiri, he tātaramoa

Kaitātaki:	Tēnā, kei hea te one matua
	Te one haumako?
Katoa:	Kei te hunga whakaaro hōhonu ki te kaupapa

Te mātātahi, te mātāpuputu
Auē! Kia kotahi noa nei te whetū
E hīnātore mai i te rangi
Te manu taupuru hei taki i te kāhui
Kātahi pea tātou ka pūreo mai
I te pōhewatanga, i te manukatanga
Te ingoingo o te ngākau taiohi e.

Leader:	*The month was January*

55

The year 1882
When Te Tūruki made his prophetic statement
To Ngāti Awa concerning its house, Rua-taupare

All: *Yes, yours is indeed a fine house*
But the only problem is, as I see it,
One wall is in conflict
With the other wall
The doorway with the back wall
The junior line with the senior line
The child with its parent

Leader: *Te Tūruki's statement continues*
All: *Looking at the contents of the house*
They are stones, sand and brambles
But the land beyond has potential

Leader: *A hundred years hence*
How do Te Tūruki's words stand?
All: *As pertinent as ever! As pertinent as ever!*
The child is in contention with its parent
The junior line with the senior
Thereby demeaning and debasing
The advice of our ancestors
For the junior line to act responsibly the senior
      line is essential
The underlying philosophy being
Mutual dependence
Not the denigrating by one
Of the other

Leader: *What is the role of the child in all this?*
All: *To remain silent, to observe and to listen*
By the time the parent passes on
The child will be mature, sturdy and robust
Never will the criticism be levelled at him
'The bungling and the incompetent
Will never aspire to the heights'
But rather
'A person taught well at home
On assuming his role on the marae, becomes it'
Leader: *This generation which is searching for*
The right example to follow
Sees, instead, at tribal gatherings
All: *When the parent stands to speak, so does the child*
When the senior line stands to speak so does the
      junior
When there's a death, the immediately bereaved

> *stand to speak*
> *Our ancestors likened this situation to*
> *The eating of food which has putrefied*

Leader: *If such is the situation, where can the young turn to?*
All: *Logically, to the marae, to the elders*
And yet those are the very places
Where ancestral advice is ignored
Yes, indeed, the contents of the house
Are stones, sand and brambles

Leader: *Where then is the land of potential fertility?*
All: *With those who give these concerns*
Their due regard
Both the young and the old
Oh, if but one star
Were to glimmer in the firmament
Or one bird were to guide the flock,
Then perhaps we would emerge
From our confusion and our anxiety
Such is the fervent desire of the young.[3]

Many Māori would say that since the arrival of the Pākehā, much of the legislation enacted has been to the detriment of the Māori. Yet a fervent, pious hope persists that all will be well if there were but mutual respect.

Kaitātaki: Ahakoa tāmia, tūkinotia iho tātou
E ngā ture, e ngā Kāwanatanga
O roto i ngā tau
Kotahi tonu te whakaaro o ngā tīpuna
Katoa: Anei rā tātou
Te papa a te mūrere
Te whakamōkeke, te whakamōkihi
Otirā e kore e whānau te pai
Ki te utua te kino ki te kino
Te taunu ki te taunu
Engari kauanuanutia ko te tangata
Te mea nui o te ao
Hei!

Leader: *Despite the repression, and our mistreatment*
By the law and governments
Over the years
Our tīpuna clung to one thought
All: *Here we are*
Victims of deceit

57

Double dealing and treachery
However, no good will accrue
If we repay malice with malice
Slander with slander
Rather, let us have respect for people
The most important thing in the world.[4]

All the haka immediately referred to were composed between 1980 and 1992.

As stated earlier, haka reflect the concerns and issues of their time. Poropeihana expresses the irritation of the people at the law of prohibition on the purchase of alcoholic liquor imposed at the behest of Sir Apirana Ngata. What the fate of those laws should be is articulated strongly. Finally, despite, in their eyes, the pernicious law, alcohol can be obtained when desired. The prohibition was imposed in 1911.

Kaea:	Ko Apirana Ngata rā te tangata
	Takarure mai rā i ngā ture
	I roto o Pōneke.
Katoa:	Horahia mai ō ture ki ahau
	Horahia mai ō ture ki ahau
	Tū ana te Minita i waenganui
	Tū ana te Minita i waenganui
	Ō ture patua ki runga ki te tekoteko
	Te whare e tū mai nei nā
Kaea:	Mahi hamupaka koia naka
Katoa:	Hei!
Kaea:	Ture Kaunihera koia naka
Katoa:	Hei!
Kaea:	Poropeihana koia naka
Katoa:	Hei!
	Ka minamina au ki te waipiro
	Ko hokona i te pō
	Hei!
Kaea:	I! Ā! hā! hā!
Katoa:	Homai ō ture kia wetewetea
	Kia wetewetea
	Hī! au!

Leader: *Apirana Ngata is the person*
              Formulating the laws in Wellington
All: *Your laws are imposed on me*
              At the centre of it all is the Minister
              Your laws will be destroyed upon the carved figure
              Of the meeting house standing here

Leader:	*Humbug is what it is*
All:	*Hei!*
Leader:	*Council laws.*
All:	*Hei!*
Leader:	*Prohibition is what is is.*
All:	*Hei!*
	I thirst for liquor and so
	I obtain it by illegal means at night
Leader:	*I Ā! hā! hā!*
All:	*Give us these laws so we may reject them*
	Reject them![5]

Tohu stated 'E kore te uku e piri ki te rino ka whitikina e te rā, ka nga-horo'. (Clay will never adhere to iron, for when the sun shines on it, it falls away.) This statement has been taken to mean that we should be who we are and not pretend to be otherwise. The haka Mangumangu Taipō is a constant reminder of this sage philosophy.

Whakarongo mai e te iwi nei
Whakarongo mai e te motu nei
Ahakoa whakapiri koe ki a tauiwi
E kore e taka te ingoa Māori i runga i a koe
He mangumangu taipō nei hoki tātou pakia!
Te kupu a Tohu ki ngā iwi e rua
'E kore e piri te uku ki te rino
Ka whitingia e te rā, ka ngahoro.'

Hearken to me, ye tribes
Hearken to me, ye land.
Whether or not you align yourself with non-Māori
The name 'Māori' will not fall from you
For we are indeed dark ghost-like creatures!
Tohu had this to say to the two peoples,
'Clay will not adhere to iron
For as soon as the sun shines on it, it will fall.'

Ngāti Tūwharetoa, occupying the shores of Lake Taupō, are the composers of the haka *I Haria*, its basic premise being that unity is essential if disaster is to be avoided.

I Haria

Kaitātaki:	I haria, i haria mai e mātou te aroha
	Ki runga i a koutou e tau nei.

Katoa:	Ā! hā! hā!
	Ā, kia kotahi mai ngā iwi nei
	Kia kotahi mai ngā iwi nei
	Hei tukituki i te rae pākira o Aituā
	Takatakahia! Takatakahia!
	Auē! Auē! Auē!
	Hei!
Leader:	*We have brought to you here assembled*
	All our affection
All:	*Ā! hā! hā!*
	Let all the tribes be united here
	To beat in the bald brow of misfortune
	Trample him underfoot, trample him underfoot
	Auē! Auē! Auē!
	Hei!

Sir James Carroll, the only person of Māori descent to have ever acted as Prime Minister of Aotearoa (for three months in 1909, and seven months in 1911), is the inspiration for the following haka by Tūhoe.

For some time the ownership of Lake Waikaremoana had been in contention, Tūhoe believing that it was theirs and Ngāti Kahungunu, the tribe of Sir James Carroll, believing that they, too, had a claim.

Sir James Carroll (1858-1926) (seated right) called on Maori to hold onto their culture. In the accompanying haka, he is bitterly criticised by Tūhoe over a land claim.

Alexander Turnbull Library

Auahi ka kā kai Pōneke rā
Kai raro iho ko Te Kāwana
Te hoa moenga i a Timi Kara
Ko te ure i tākaia nei ki te rau o te nōti
Tiaia mai hoki ki te rau o te hiriwa
Kia pai ai koe te kai i te whenua e
I! Ā! hā! hā!

Tono tuatahi nā Te Kārimana
Kia tukua atu te rūri mō te rohe pōtae
Ka hoki atu taku mihi ki te urunga tapu
Kai raro iho ko te ope hōia
Hai hopu i ahau ki te whare herehere
Kāti māku ko te whakahoki i ngā mahi kikino a te Kāwana
E patu nei i taku whenua nei
I! Ā! hā! hā!

Ehara taku mana i te mana hou
He mana tawhito tonu taku mana
Rūrū rawa mai, ka rūrū mai
Ka mahora ngā ture ki te urunga tapu
E ai te kauika pakake,
Inā te Tūruki kai Te Wainui
Peke mai anō ko Te Kāwana
Ki te kohi atu i te roi a Tūhoe
Hai roi mō tana whenua, mō Ruatāhuna
Kai pau i te whānako nei, i a Timi Kara
Pāiri taku poho e!

Smoke rises above Wellington
Beneath it is the Governor
Bedmate of James Carroll
Whose penis is wrapped with hundreds of notes
And studded with many pieces of silver
So that my land can be consumed with ease
Ā! hā! hā!

The first request came from Cadman
For the territory to be surveyed
I address my compliments to my sacred natal soil
Where the troops of soldiers are located
To take me to prison
My only recourse is to react
To the evil deeds of the Governor
Who is destroying my land

I! Ā! hā! hā!

My authority over this territory is not recent
It is an ancient authority
A hand is offered in friendship
Yet laws continue to be imposed on my natal soil
Numerous as a school of whales
Te Tūruki takes up residence at Te Wainui
Once more the Governor intervenes
Taking to himself the rich resources of Tūhoe
Let us assemble all our resources at Ruatāhuna
Lest claim be laid to them by this thief, James Carroll.
How this saddens me! 6

Pre-contact haka are still included in the repertoire of many tribes but the occasions on which they are performed are fewer because the reasons for their having been composed are no longer appropriate in today's context. While not performed as often, they are still remembered.

---

1 Kāretu, Timoti S. *Ngā waiata me ngā haka a te kapa haka o Te Whare Wānanga o Waikato.* pp. 17-20. Hamilton, University of Waikato, 1992.

2 Ibid.

3 Ibid. pp. 27-30.

4 Ibid. pp. 33-34.

5 Dewes, Te Kapunga, ed. *Māori literature: He haka taparahi: men's ceremonial dance-poetry.* p. 19. Wellington, Department of Anthropology, Victoria University of Wellington, 1972.

6 From a collection of Tūhoe haka and chants held by the author.

6

KA MATE, KA MATE
THE MOST CELEBRATED
OF HAKA

As is the case with haka, waiata-ā-ringa and waiata which become common property there are minor variations in the lyric.

The following version and translation of Te Rauparaha's ngeri, *Ka Mate*, is that given by the late Dr Pei Te Hurinui Jones, noted Māori scholar, in his book *Pōtatau*.

Ka mate, Ka mate

Kikiki!
Kokoko!
Kei waniwania taku hika;
Kei tara-wahia!
Kei te rua i te karokaro
He pounga rahui!
He uira ki te rangi!
Ketekete mai hoki to poro kai-riri;
'Mau au, e Koro, e?
'I a, ka wehi au, ka mataku!'
Ko wai te tangata kia rere ure?
Tirohanga nga rua rerarera
Hei a kuri ka kamukamu

Ka mate! Ka mate!
Ka ora! Ka ora!
Tenei te tangata puhuruhuru
Nana nei te tiki mai
I whakawhiti te ra!
Upane! Upane!
Upane! Ka upane!
Whiti te ra!

Solo:	*Let your valour arise!*
	Let your temper rage!
Chorus:	*We'll ward off the desecrating touch;*
	We'll ward off the impious hand;
	We'll ne'er let the foe

	Outrage our cherished ones!
	We'll guard our women and our maidens;
	And be thou, O Leader, our boundary Pillar!

Solo: *For ye all, I'll defy the lightning of the Heavens!*
Chorus: *The foe, he will stand frustrated;*
             In his mad and impotent rage!

Solo: *Mine ears will then be spared*
             The maidens' despairing cry
             'Will ye, O Sir, possess me?
             The thought it makes me quail'
Chorus: *Who, in his manhood will stand affrighted;*
             Or in his terror, flee?
             For he will surely perish
             And in the refuse pit will lie
             As food for dogs to gnaw with relish!

Solo: *Avaunt, O Death! Avaunt, O Death!*
Chorus: *Ah, 'tis life! 'tis life!*
             Behold!! There stands the hairy man
             Who will cause the sun to shine!

Solo: *One upward step! Another upward step!*
Chorus: *One last upward step;*
             Then step forth!
             Into the Sun
             The Sun that shines!

Thus Te Rauparaha exhorted Ngāti Toa to fight as they had never fought before. They were feeling the unrelenting pressure being exerted on them by Te Wherowhero, the first Māori king, and his invading army of Waikato. The situation had been brought about by the killing of a number of high-born people of Waikato who were out to wreak vengeance and to rid the territory of Te Rauparaha and his people of Ngāti Toa once and for all.

It was as a consequence of this that Te Rauparaha with Ngāti Toa and Ngāti Raukawa moved south to Kapiti Island, where they were able to escape the wrath of Waikato but where Te Rauparaha continued to wage battle against the tribes of the south.

When the high chief Hape, of Ngāti Raukawa, lay dying he asked who would take his place. None of his three sons answered, even though he repeated the question. It might well have been the solemnity and sadness of the occasion, or they might have considered it inappropriate to make a response.

Te Rauparaha, however, exhibited no such reticence and each time the chief Hape asked his question Te Rauparaha replied that he would

E Abbott
June 1845.

TE RAUPARAHA.

Te Rauparaha, the famous warrior-chief of Ngati Toa, composed and performed the most celebrated of all haka, 'Ka mate, ka mate'. This sketch by E. I. Abbott dates from 1845.

assume the reins of leadership in the high chief Hape's stead. And so Te Rauparaha became leader of Ngāti Toa, although on his mother Pare-kōhatu's side he claimed Ngāti Raukawa descent.

It was in the year 1821 that Te Rauparaha and his people migrated south to occupy Kapiti Island, and the areas known today as Levin, Ōtaki and south to Porirua.

Prior to his enforced departure Te Rauparaha had tried to recruit an army to overthrow Waikato but his requests for support were declined by Te Arawa, to whom he could claim affiliation. His companions returned home but he decided to continue on to try to persuade Ngāti Tūwharetoa of Taupō to his cause. He could also claim affiliation to Tūwharetoa and thought that by using taunting remarks he might irritate them into supporting him, but to no avail. Many of the hapū of Ngāti Tūwharetoa were not kindly disposed to him because of his behaviour on a previous visit.

Asking the chief Te Rore to accompany him, Te Rauparaha decided to visit the paramount chief of Ngāti Tūwharetoa, Te Heuheu, at Te Rapa. En route, however, they found Ngāti Te Aho, a sub-tribe of

Ngāti Tūwharetoa, waiting to kill him in revenge for having suffered at his hands some years before.

Te Rore and Te Rauparaha were forced to Rangatira and from there travelled by canoe to Te Rapa in the hope that they would be protected by Te Heuheu. Such was not to be but he advised them to travel on to the chief Te Wharerangi who, he asssured them, would give them refuge.

Upon their arrival they found Te Wharerangi's people equally hostile to him, but since Te Heuheu had guaranteed him his safety Te Wharerangi felt obligated to offer Te Rauparaha protection. Te Wharerangi indicated a pit to Te Rauparaha and told him to conceal himself in it.

Te Wharerangi's wife, Te Rangikoaea, was asked to sit over the entrance. The chiefs of the pursuing party soon arrived and began reciting chants in an endeavour to locate Te Rauparaha's whereabouts. The chants indicated he was at Motuopuhi, and to prevent his escaping southwards further chants were recited. In the meantime Te Rauparaha, concealed in the pit, began to realise that the spells were having an effect on him.

Let Sir John Te Herekiekie Grace take up the account in his book *Tūwharetoa*:

Now, in addition to assisting in the concealment of the Ngati Toa chief, the main reason why Te Rangikoaea was ordered to sit over the pit was because of the neutralising effect that she as a woman had on incantations. The genital organs were supposed to have this strange power and as the incantations reached Te Rauparaha he felt their effects being neutralised by the chieftainess sitting above him. He imagined them being whirled round and round and being absorbed, and to give vent to his feelings he exclaimed,

> Aha ha!
> Kikiki kakaka kauana!
> Kei waniwania taku tara.
> Kei tarawahia, kei te rua i te kerokero!

After a while he realised that the protecting powers of the chieftainess could be destroyed if certain advances were made by her husband and that in order to save himself he would have to be watchful and see that his protector was not disturbed. Becoming concerned, he whispered,

> 'He pounga rahui te uira ka rarapa;
> Ketekete kauana to peru kairiri.
> Mau au e koro e
> Hi! Ha!
> Ka wehi au ka matakana.
> Ko wai te tangata kia rere ure?

Tirohanga nga rua rerarera
Nga rua kuri kakanui i raro!'

When the pursuers arrived they enquired of Te Wharerangi whether he had seen Te Rauparaha and were informed that he had fled in the direction of the Rangipo desert. For a moment they did not believe him, but later hurried off in pursuit. When all was clear Te Wharerangi asked his wife to let Te Rauparaha out.

During the time Tauteka was talking to Te Wharerangi, Te Rauparaha muttered under his breath, 'Aha ha! Ka mate, ka mate!' (Aha ha! I die, I die!), but when the Rotoaira chief indicated that the man they sought had gone to Rangipo he murmured, 'Ka ora, ka ora!' (I live, I live!) However, when Tauteka doubted Te Wharereangi he gloomily muttered, 'Ka mate, ka mate!' (I die, I die!) Then, when his pursuers were convinced he was not in Te Wharerangi's pa but had made for Taranaki he exclaimed, 'Ka ora, ka ora! Tenei te tangata puhuruhuru nana nei i tiki mai whakawhiti te ra!' (I live, I live! For this is the hairy man who has fetched the sun and caused it to shine again!) As he took his first two steps out of the pit he said, 'Hupane, kaupane!' and as he stood clear he shouted, 'Whiti te ra!' (The sun shines!)

Going on to the courtyard of Te Wharerangi and before Te Rangikoaea and the assembled people, Te Rauparaha performed his famous haka.

> Aha ha!
> Kikiki kakaka kauana!
> Kei waniwania taku tara.
> Kei tarawahia, kei te rua i te kerokero!
> He pounga rahui te uira ka rarapa
> Ketekete kau ana to peru kairiri
> Mau au e koro e
> Hi! Ha!
> Ka wehi au ka matakana,
> Ko wai te tangata kia rere ure?
> Tirohanga nga rua rerarera
> Nga rua kuri kakanui i raro!
> Aha ha!
> A, ka mate! ka mate!
> Ka ora, ka ora!
> Ka mate! ka mate!
> Ka ora, ka ora
> Tenei te tangata puhuruhuru
> Nana nei i tiki mai whakawhiti te ra!
> Hupane! Kaupane!
> Whiti te ra!

The haka is well-known to this day and is heard in every Maori settlement throughout New Zealand. Some tribes dispute the origin described above, but none has been able to put forward any explanation of how it came into being as Ngati Toa and Ngati Tuwharetoa have done in this account.

Ka Mate has since become the most performed, the most maligned, the most abused of all haka, although it was, originally, a ngeri and is often performed as such.

Many sports teams and individuals travelling from Aotearoa abroad tend to include *Ka Mate* in their repertoires as an indication of their place of origin. Perhaps the team that has given *Ka Mate* its greatest exposure abroad and in Aotearoa, has been the All Blacks, who perform it before every fixture. Their reception varies from country to country but it has become a distinctive feature of Aotearoa's premier rugby team.

Ka Mate is also the haka favoured by many secondary schools that do not have haka groups. In a number of these cases, if not the majority, the words are bowdlerised, mispronounced and it is obvious that no cognisance is taken of the lyric and what it might be trying to say.

One of the main features that has been incorporated into this haka by non-Māori groups is the jumping at the end. Jumping is not a feature of either haka taparahi or ngeri and it is these irritating perpetrations which lead to a lot of discord. The He Taua incident at the University of Auckland in 1978-79 is an index of the frustration that many Māori people feel at the continued demeaning and debasing of haka by the ignorant.

While *Ka Mate* will continue to be performed by many who know nothing of its background or its meaning, it can still send a chill up the spine when performed spontaneously by a host of people who might be using it to welcome guests, to endorse remarks made by orators or to give vent to strong feelings.

It is the most celebrated of all haka and will always have appeal to the Māori for reasons far different from those of the non-Māori. While many haka are ephemeral, *Ka Mate* persists and will linger on while there are people to perform it and who care about the art of haka.

7

HAKA TODAY

It seemed to me that such a publication as this could not be contemplated without canvassing the opinions of some of the people actively involved in the performance, composition and retention of haka. Hāmuera Mitchell, doyen of haka, from Rotorua, had this to say when asked for his opinion of haka today.

Ki a au nei hā, kua ngaro te wairua Māori o ngā kaumātua o mua, te mana, te ihi me te mataku. Mā te aha kei te mau tonu. Engari ko ētahi o ngā wāhi tapu kei te tino ngaro haere. Ko te tū tonu o te tāne me te tū tika, me maranga te uma, kauaka e tūohu. Kia māro ngā ringa, kia kori te tinana, ka hūpeke ngā waewae, kia tika te takahi o te waewae, te aroarohaki o ngā ringaringa, te whētero, te pūkana, te pīkarikari o te kanohi. Ko te tū riri tonu o te tinana mai i te māhunga tae noa ki ngā raparapa waewae hou atu ki ngā matimati. Tāpiri atu hoki ki te kotahi o te hāparangi o ngā reo o te kapa haka. E hika mau ana te wehiwehi. Ki a au nei, kei ngā kaitakitaki kei ngā kaiwhakahaere o ngā kapa haka hoki tētahi wāhi nui hei whakawana, hei whakaoho i te kapa haka a ngā tāne, ā, tae noa ki ngā manu ngangahu hei taotao, hei whāngai haere i ngā taha.

In my opinion, the Māori spirit of our elders has been lost. The passion, the excitement and the instilling of fear. Let's be thankful for small mercies, the haka is still alive. However, some of the more essential features are in decline. The male stance is one, he should stand erect, the back should be straight, not stooped, the hands should be firm, the body should be supple, the feet should stamp, the feet should stamp properly, the hands should quiver, the tongue protrude, the eyes dilate, the face be expressive. The body should adopt an aggressive stance, from the head to the soles of the feet, including the fingers. In concert with this, the voices of the group should be loud. Should such be the case, how awesome!

I feel that the leaders and tutors of the haka groups have a crucial role in bringing their groups alive including the manu ngangahu whose function is to perform to either side of the group.[1]

Hāmuera Mitchell, or Hamu, as he is affectionately known throughout the Māori world, is of another era and yet what he has to say is still pertinent and cogent. A contemporary of his, the late Venerable Archeacon Sir Kīngi Īhaka, chairman of the Aotearoa Māori Performing Arts Festival, had this to say when asked for his opinion on the state of contemporary haka:

Atareta Maxwell collection

Hāmuera Mitchell, elder of the tribes of Te Arawa, addressing the assembly on the marae on the occasion of the investiture of Sir Howard Morrison. Hāmuera Mitchell is one of the few older masters of haka still living, and has very definite ideas about what haka should be.

Taku mōhio i a mātou e tamariki ana kāre ngā wāhine e haka tahi ana me ngā tāne, nā rā, haka taparahi. Taku mōhio ka tū ngā tāne ki te haka, he tāne rawa ngā ringaringa, ngā tikanga, ngā waewae, te hiki o te waewae, ērā āhua mahi katoa. Ko ngā wāhine kei muri kē. Ka mutu tonu tā te wahine he pūkana, engari kāre e kōrero ana i nga kupu o te haka, kāre e āwhina haere ana, e tautoko ana i ngā tāne mō te haka. Waihongia ai tērā mā ngā tāne anake. Ā, i nāianei ka mātaki-taki au ki ā tātou mahi engari kua puta aku whakaaro, ko au ake, kāore au e taunga ana ki ērā tikanga e ka tīoro mai te reo wahine i te taha o te tāne ka riro kē, nui kē te waha o te wahine i tō ngā tāne, koirā taku wehi ki ētahi o ā tātou, taku whakahē rā ki ētahi o ā tātou mahi. Ka riro kē mā ngā wāhine e hiki te haka. Pōhēhē ana au, āe, ōku nei whakaaro kei te hē, ōku ake mā ngā tāne anō e hiki. Whakaaengia ana pea kia tautokongia e ngā wāhine engari kaua e pērā rawa te kaha o ngā reo, e, kia riro anō nei ko ngā wāhine kē nga kaitātaki o te haka, koirā taku āwangawanga ki ngā haka o nāianei.

I am positive that when we were young, women did not perform the haka with the men, that is, in haka taparahi. In my opinion, when men perform haka, their actions are too masculine, the conventions, the stamping of the feet, the way the foot is lifted, all those aspects. The women were to the rear. The sole function of the women was to pūkana, but they did not say the words of the haka, they did not help the men vocally. That was the exclusive domain of the men.

Today, as I watch our performances, the thought occurs to me: I, personally, am not accustomed to the practice of women's voices

Vince Heperi

The late Sir Kīngi Matutaera Īhaka, inaugural Chairman of the Aotearoa Maori Performing Arts Festival Committee. Sir Kīngi was critical of many of the innovations in contemporary haka.

calling out the lyric along with the men. In some instances the women's voices are louder than those of the men. This is one of my concerns, and why I disapprove of this aspect of our performance. It is left to the women to give voice to the haka. I was beginning to think that I was mistaken. It is the function of the men to give voice to the haka. Perhaps, women are permitted vocal support. But not for their voices to predominate, as though it is the women who are leading the haka. That is my greatest concern about haka today.[2]

When the same question was posed to Ngāpō Wehi, leader and tutor of Wakahuia, winners of the 1985 and 1992 Aotearoa Māori Performing Arts Festivals, his response was as follows:

Heoi anō kia mōhio tāua ko tēnei mea te haka i mua, haka i runga i te marae he rerekē i nāianei. I aua rā, e rua ngā wae pērā, pīrangi koe ki te hiki i ō waewae ka hikina e koe, nō i nāianei nā te mea kāore e kitea me pēhea e whakawāngia ai ngā rōpū, ko te nuinga o ngā rōpū kua takahi waewae kē, kotahi te waewae takahi i nāianei koirā pea te hē o ēnei mahi, mehemea he hē kei roto nā, kua whakaritea tātou katoa. Heoi anō kei te ako tonu ahau engari i kite au i ngā tohunga o ēnei mahi i roto o Te Aitanga-a-Māhaki, o Ngāti Porou nō reira nāku i hamuhamu haere tēnei mea o te tū o te tangata, he rerekē hoki a Ngāti Porou.

71

We should be aware that haka formerly was performed on the marae. It is different today. In those days there were two feet that stamped, if you wanted to lift your foot you lifted it. Today because it is difficult to find aspects whereby groups can be judged, the majority of the groups have a different foot action. Only one foot stamps now. That is probably what is wrong, if, in fact it is wrong. We are becoming uniform. However I am still teaching but I saw the experts in haka of Te Aitanga-a-Māhaki and Ngāti Porou and so I gleaned what I could regarding the stance because Ngāti Porou has a different stance.[3]

Horowaewae Maxwell, leader of Ngāti Rangiwewehi, winners in 1983 and one of the Aotearoa's top groups from Rotorua, had this to say,

Well, I find it exciting if I can reflect on the one we've just done previously at Ngāruawāhia. It was a tremendous change for us. It was actually, it was the tutors, like Ātareta and I having to step back because we sort of gave everything to our young leader, young Hiwaroa and said we'll support him all the way and he came up with the thought of perhaps portraying Rangi and Papa. We sort of scratched our heads and thought how? He gave his thoughts to Uenuku Fairhall and Uenuku worked on the words. He worked on the actions and asked us for our approval and we looked at it and we were just over the moon with what he came up with and I guess it's allowing young people to come up with their ideas. Then we looked at it and we thought, you know, it's a risk, do we do it? It mightn't come off in front of judges, who might be fixed in their ways about certain traditional things and we thought, let's run with it. We're very pleased we did. Okay, we got approval from two of the judges. One said we were in the year 2000, which hurt, but at the same time we felt good inside that we were doing something that was innovative, creative, new but still had an old kaupapa, Rangi and Papa.

Despite the creativity of the haka of Ngāti Rangiwewehi he still had some reservations:

Yes, but it's always a worry in the back of our minds. All the judges approve of what you do and when you get two very high marks and one very low mark it hurts but it was really thrilling to see the development of this haka and seeing the boys portraying it and I said earlier in our meeting this is the first time in all the festivals we've been to that we've allowed the women to come in, in any form, any shape and form, and they came in with their voices when we portrayed the separation of Rangi and Papa and we really felt good about it and we often have our friends say to us, they felt really good about what we did and we certainly did.

Seeing our boys on their backs and kicking their feet in the air and to me I think this is what the festival's all about. With twenty-eight teams we can't possibly all be doing the same haka or style, you know, so I'd like to think that we've had the courage to try and do something new.[4]

This innovative aspect of Ngāti Rangiwewehi's haka prompted Sir Kīngi Īhaka to state:

Kua kore i haka. Kua pēhea kē rānei ētahi o ngā kupu, he aha rā te take? Huri ake anō, huri ake anō, ko aua kōrero anō. Kāre rawa atu nei he hōhonutanga o ngā kupu, ā, ngā tāne ka tuwhera mai ngā waewae, ka hinga ki raro, ka whakatāhinga i a rātou, ka whanawhana mai, ka aha mai, e tā!

They are no longer performing haka. What are the words trying to convey, what is the point? Ad nauseam, the composers use the same lyric, the lyric has no depth, and as for the men, they open their legs wide, become limp, they kick from the ground and so on. Goodness gracious me![5]

Ngāti Rangiwewehi's haka depicted the separation of Rangi (Sky Father) and Papa (Earth Mother). The haka started with the men on their backs and their feet in the air, a most uconventional feature of haka, hence Sir Kīngi's comment.

As a consequence of both the haka of Ngāti Rangiwewehi and Tūhourangi of Rotorua, who used the legend of Hatupatu and Kurangaituku as the theme for their composition, I asked the question, 'Where do you see the haka going?' It should be noted that many of the people observing the aforementioned haka were quite strongly of the opinion that they were not haka in the accepted, conventional sense but more akin to play-acting.

My question elicited the following response from Te Horowaewae:

I hope it's allowed to be creative without being told that a judge is going to judge you from a traditional base because we are actu-ally wrestling with this original composition thing which is mak-ing a lot of our haka oncers because we can't perform them again.

Ngāpō's response was:

Kāre au i te tino mōhio me pēhea taku whakahoki i tēnā kōrero. Heoi anō ki a au nei, he haka tētahi mea ana he kōrero kei roto. Koirā kē tāku e whai nei. Ka rite anō ki ngā kōrero me āhei ki te kaupapa ngā kupu, ngā ringa. Nā koirā taku mahi nui kia rite pērā nā te mea ētahi o ngā rōpū he rerekē ngā kōrero, he rerekē ngā ringa. Nō reira, ka kitea atu ātaahua, engari ko ngā tāngata e mōhio ana kāre i ōrite. Kāre i rerekē atu i a au ngā mahi. Ko te kupu te mea nui, kāore ko te rangi, ko te rangi he mea kawe noa iho i te kōrero koirā noa iho.

I don't quite know how to respond to that question. However, as far as I'm concerned, haka is something which has a message. That is what I am pursuing. It is like what has already been said, the theme, the lyric and the actions should be compatible. That is my principal task — to ensure that that occurs, because with some groups the theme is different and the actions are different. It is nice to look at but people who know the art of haka are not uniform in movement. I am no different. The lyric is the most important aspect, not the rhythm or tune. The tune is purely a vehicle for the lyric, that is all.

In response to the same question Sir Kīngi said:

Kua āhua ōrite katoa ngā haka o nāianei, koirā taku wehi. Taku hiahia hoki mehemea ka taea e tēnā rōpū, e tēnā takiwā, ā rātou ake haka kaua e whai i ngā haka a ētahi kē atu, ki konā pekepeke ai mō te pekepeke noa iho te take. Koirā anō au i kōhete ai ki ā ⁻tātou rōpū. Te mate hoki ko ngā tāngata kaha ki te pekepeke, ko ngā tāngata ērā e pakipakingia ana.

All the haka today look the same, that's what worries me. It is my wish, if it is possible, for each group or district to perform their own haka, not to emulate the haka of others, incorporating jumping just for the sake of jumping. That is why I castigate our groups. The problem is, the groups who jump a great deal are those who are most applauded.

Te Hāmana Mahuika when commenting on the foot action in haka had this to say:

Mō te takahi o te waewae. Ki tā te Māori kotahi tonu te takahi o te waewae. Kei reira te tohungatanga o te kaitātaki haka ki te tāima i ngā kupu kia haere i runga i te takahi o te waewae.

Ko te takahi o te waewae o ētahi o tēnei whakatipuranga e rua rawa ngā waewae. Kua rite i tēnā wā ki tā te Hawaiana ki te hura rānei. Nō reira tāu, tā te Māori, kia kotahi te whiu o te waewae.

With regard to the foot action, according to the Māori only one foot stamps. This is how the brilliance of the leader can be seen when he times his words to coincide with the stamping of the foot.

Vince Heperi

Ngāpō Wehi, leader and tutor of Wakahuia (Auckland) and former leader and tutor of Waihīrere (Gisborne). Ngāpō and his wife Pīmia have tutored groups who have, between them, won the aggregate trophy at the Aotearoa Maori Performing Arts Festival four times. No other tutors have been as successful. It is a tribute to their love of, and their dedication to, the Maori performing arts.

> *The foot action of some of today's generation is to lift both feet. They are similar to Hawai'ians, to the movements in hula. Yours, that of the Māori, is for only one foot to be lifted.*

It is interesting to note that many haka men do tend to lift both feet, a very distracting feature, while others lift neither foot. The lifting of the foot is one of the most elementary features of haka. If the dust is to be stirred, an essential feature of haka, then the foot must be lifted.

The whole aspect of stance was expressed thus by Ngāpō Wehi:

Heoi anō ko te tū tuatahi, kaua e tino whānui ngā waewae, kaua e tino tata, nā me kī rā, te whānui o ngā pakihiwi i reira, anā ko te heke ki raro kei a koe tēnā. Ko ngā tāne tāroaroa nei me heke ki raro, ko ngā mea potopoto nei kāre e tino heke ki raro kia rite ai.

75

Koirā noa iho me te tū whakahīhī nei kia mōhio ai rātou i roto i ō rātou whakaaro he aha te tū o ō rātou tīpuna i mua, koirā kē. Me whakaaro e rātou tērā, pēnā ka whakaritea e au ki ngā tekoteko me ngā poupou nei. Ko ērā tū tōtika tonu kāre e whati te tuarā engari me pērā. Ko ngā ringa kaua e rite ki te waiata-ā-ringa nei, ngā kupu me whakatuma haere koirā noa iho.

Firstly the stance — the legs should not be too far apart, nor too close together, let's say perhaps about shoulder width. How low you go is up to you. Tall men need to sink quite low, the shorter ones not quite so far so that there's some uniformity. That's all as well as standing proud so that they will know in their minds what the stance of their ancestors was, that really is the reason. They must bear that in mind. I compare them to the poupou and tekoteko in the meeting house. I tell them that they stand erect, the back is not bent, the actions should not be as they are in waiata-ā-ringa, the words should be staccato-like, that is all.

Horowaewae Maxwell:

Well, put it this way, yes, we do have a definite style, it's different from Ngāti Porou. We do not stoop as low. Further on I like to think it's a Te Arawa influence when Irirangi came into our group then he instilled another kind of influence where he then started to make the men shake, the arms and bodies and heads and various things. We did a haka in Hastings, Unumia, which did a lot of the shaking which now I see a lot of the groups have adopted. So I guess that's another style to add.

Sir Kīngi Īhaka:

Ko te tū o te tangata. Tū tangata, tū tāne, kaua e tū wahine mai. Pai noa iho te heke whakararo engari kia kitea atu ngā kanohi. Pai noa iho tērā kaha o te heke engari ko muri o te ūpoko kaua e kitea atu. E kia kite tonu atu koe i te kanohi o te tangata. Kāre pea he hē o te heke. Me takahi, me takahi te waewae kia āhua turituri ai pea, kia aha ai rānei? Āe, kia kino nei hoki, kia tika ai hoki te rangi o te haka. Ki te kore hoki e takahi te waewae ka kotiti rātou.

The stance. Adopt a masculine stance, don't be feminine. It's permissible to sink low but the eyes must be seen. It's fine to sink really low but the back of the head should not be seen — you should see the performer's face. The foot should stamp, sufficiently to be heard. The foot should be stamped quite loudly so that the haka is performed better. If the foot is not stamped the beat of the haka can be lost.

The question to be asked now is, 'Is haka in a healthy state?'

Horowaewae Maxwell says:

Yes, the discussion of having women involved. I personally would like the men to be judged as doing the haka. I think it's in a fairly healthy state, except we should be allowed to do our haka that have been done before.

As will have been noted earlier, Horowaewae is supported by Sir Kīngi Īhaka with regard to the place of women in haka. It certainly does not coincide with what was noted by early observers of haka or with Ngāpō's comment on this aspect regarding his father's sister, Rāwinia Wehi, a renowned haka woman.

He tika tāu, i kite hoki au i a ia i Rūātoki e noho ana mātou i roto i te wharenui i reira, i Tūmatauenga. Kī atu au ki a ia, he haka anō te wahine i mua. Ka tū mai a ia, ana i te wharenui rā me te papaki i tana poho, ngā taonga katoa.

Āe, tino tau rawa atu. Ko ētahi o ngā mea i mau i a au engari kei te hoki anō au ki te kōrero kei te āhua pōuri au nā te mea kāore au i tino noho i tana taha.

You are correct, because I saw her when she was in Rūātoki and we were assembled in the house Tūmatauenga. I asked her if women performed haka in days gone by. She stood up slapping her chest and displayed all the essentials of haka.

Yes, she was a beautiful performer. Some things I was able to learn from her but I return to an earlier comment where I said I am sorry I did not really spend more time with her.

The contemporary tendency is to be over-expressive, to exaggerate the movements, to be overt rather than subtle, to reveal all rather than to let the mind and the imagination be stimulated. Sir Kīngi Īhaka's reservations with regard to lyric, theme and performance were expressed thus:

Ko ngā kupu o roto, kāore au e tino mārama ana he aha te take i pērā rawa ai. Ko ētahi pēnei tonu i te kōrero kanga nei. Ko ētahi e whakaputa ana i ngā kōrero mō te mate tāne, mate wahine, ērā tū momo kōrero katoa i roto i te haka. Pai noa iho pea i mua, engari i nāianei pōhēhē ana au kua kore katoa ērā āhuatanga i waenganui i a tātou. Kua rite tonu tātou ki ngā wā o te kai tangata.

I am not certain why some of the lyrics are the way they are. Some are tantamount to cursing, others are obsessed with sexual intercourse, all such like themes are in haka. I suppose that's all

Vince Heperi

Horowaewae Maxwell and his wife Ātareta, tutor and leaders of Ngāti Rangiwewehi (Rotorua).

right, but today I thought we had abandoned all such practices. We have returned to the time when we were cannibals.

The question then posed was, 'Do you think things have gone too far in that direction?' Sir Kīngi's response was:

Kua kaha rawa, kua kaha rawa te pērā, ki a au rā. Me te mea nei, ā, mā ngā haka rā e ora ai tātou, nā, ētahi o ngā kupu o ngā haka nei, tū mai ki te haka, tuwhera mai ngā hūhā o ngā wāhine, o nga tāne. Kei te hē ki a au ērā tikanga, ki ahau ake.

Too far, far too far, in my opinion. It's as though we think we will survive because of haka, so some of the lyrics would have it. When they arise to perform the women and the men open their legs wide. I, personally, find such a stance abhorrent.

Apart from the concerns expressed, haka is considered to be in a healthy state.

[1] Personal correspondence to the author, dated 7 September 1991.

[2] Taped interview at the Waipuna Hotel, Auckland, 23 March 1992.

[3] Ngāpō Wehi interviewed by the author.

[4] Horowaewae Maxwell interviewed by the author.

[5] Sir Kīngi Īhaka interviewed by the author.

8

HAKA AND COMPETITION

It has already been stated that the haka is very much alive and enjoying the popularity with both performer and audience that it has always had. Of the Māori dance repertoire it can be said that the haka is the most eagerly anticipated wherever there is a performance.

The Aotearoa Māori Performing Arts Festival, formerly known as the Polynesian Festival, has played a major role in the raising of the standard of performance of haka and ensuring that a high standard is maintained.

The principal function of this festival, as conceived by the Māori visionaries and luminaries of the early 1970s, was to raise the standard of performance for, primarily, tourist consumption and to provide an incentive for tribes to actively revive the traditional chant and haka of their own areas. That the festival has succeeded in so doing no one would be churlish enough to deny; in fact one could state quite categorically that the dreams of those early visionaries, many of whom are no longer with us, have, to a certain extent, been realised.

The national committee that comprises delegates from the different areas designated, initially, by the Māori Land Court with others being added later, is responsible for policy pertaining to the festival. It is a misnomer to call it a festival when it is actually a competition, one of the compulsory items, along with poi, action song and traditional chant, being the haka.

Rules for judges and competitors are determined by these delegates after much discussion and quite often heated debate. The guidelines have changed over the years depending on the whims of the delegates but, at present, there is an element of common sense prevailing.

Some of the rules stipulated by the delegates have been contentious and controversial and have been fiercely contested by some of the groups. It is fortunate that some groups have been vociferous in stating their objections, thus forcing the delegates back to the drawing board to reconsider some of the rules thought by the groups to be nonsensical or ill-founded.

One such policy was the banning of females from the haka. Many groups refused to abide by this decision of the national committee and gave vent to their spleen in song and haka, the following song exemplifying the anger and frustration of one of the competing groups:

Pupū ake ana i taku whatu manawa
Te whakatakariri me te pōuri nui
Ki te hunga e whakahaere nei,

Vince Heperi

The crews of the canoes of Turangawaewae, as hosts of the 1992 festival, prepare to welcome and honour their guests with a haka.

Whakatakoto ture tikanga kore,
Mō ngā mahi nei mahi tauwhāinga
E tautokohia nei e ngā kapa puta noa
Inā hoki i kīia mai ahau
Kaua te wahine e haka i te taha o te tāne
Ki te whērā, he kore take
He kore take nō te tāne e
Ka kimikimi ko te hinengaro
Ka pātai te ngākau he aha kē
Te tino kaupapa o ngā mahi nei
Āe rānei he whakahau i te rangatahi
Ki te pupuri i ngā taonga hirahira
I heke mai i ngā huihuinga, kāwaitanga
Āe rānei he takatakahi
I ngā mana, i ngā wehi o ngā iwi
Horouta te waka – he haka te wahine!
Te Arawa te waka – he haka te wahine!
Mātaatua te waka - he haka te wahine!
Te kaupapa kē he tautoko, he āwhina
He whakahau tā te wahine i te tāne,
Kia puta ai te wana, te ihi, te wehi
Hei hoa mō te tau o te kupu
Ngā tino taonga o roto i ēnei mahi
Ki te kore hoki he aha te aha?
Nō Tua-whakarere te tikanga e mau nei i ahau

81

Nā rātou mā hoki ēnei kupu ōhākī
'Auaka tumutumu te kura i Awarua.'
Tihē! Tihē! mauri ora!

From the very depths of my being wells up
Anger and resentment
At the attitude of the organising body
Who make pointless rules
For these competitions
Which have the support of groups throughout the country.
For I have been told
That the women must not haka with the men
And should they persist in so doing
It is tantamount to saying that the men are useless
The mind wonders
And the soul searches
For the philosophy underlying these activities
Is it to encourage the younger generation,
To retain those valued items
Which exist as a consequence of the gatherings of experts,
Or is it to brazenly ignore
The practices and customs of other tribes?
In the territory of Horouta canoe — women haka!
In the territory of Te Arawa canoe — women haka!
In the territory of Mātaatua canoe — women haka!
The philosophy really is that the women should support, boost,
And give encouragement to the men,
So that the excitement, vigour and panache will merge
As an accompaniment for the lyrics
Which are, after all, the most important aspects of these activities.
Should they be absent from the performance, then what is the point?
The custom which I am observing has come down through the ages
And it was they, our ancestors, who left this advice
'Do not forsake the customs whose origins are in Awarua'.
Tihē mauri ora![1]

Traditionally, female performed with male in the haka,

After each of my retinue were presented to the chief, partaking of
the honour of the hongi, or salutation, the haka, or dance of welcome, was performed; this was commenced by our entertainers,
who placed themselves in an extended line, in ranks four deep.
This dance, to a stranger witnessing it for the first time, is calcu-
lated to excite the most alarming fears; the entire body of performers, male and female, free and bond, were mixed together,
without reference to the rank they held in the community.[2]

It was ironic at this particular festival, in 1980 in Auckland, that two of the women judges performed a haka just to make the point to the national committee that they really were not being endorsed by either the judges or majority of the performing groups. It could be truly said that this policy of the national committee was one of its most unpopular and deserved to be rejected.

All Māori forms of dance need both male and female as they are complementary to each other except that in the haka the male is to the fore, in the poi the female is to the fore, in the traditoinal chant both are to the fore with the female being to the fore in the action song. The performance is lack-lustre without both elements fully contributing.

While the national committee does stipulate what judges should observe, the final decision is left to the judges, who are selected by the delegates from the nominations received from the different areas. It is accepted that the judges are selected because they are able to exemplify what they have been nominated to judge, they are speakers of the language and are conversant with the different conventions that pertain from tribal group to tribal group. Judges need to verge on the omnipotent to be really acceptable – theirs is an unenviable and unappreciated task!

Over the last two decades or so that the festival has been in existence, the haka has reached a very high standard and one wonders whether there are further heights still to be scaled. One of the dreams of the visionaries that has not been fully realised is the revival of classical haka. The groups of Ngāti Porou, more than any other, confine themselves to the classics of their own repertoire, but most of the groups have set about composing new haka, thus adding to the repertoire.

There are very few groups competing who are truly tribal – probably no more than five out of the twenty-eight to thirty groups. It is therefore not really surprising that groups have opted for their own compositions as many of these groups comprise people from all the tribes.

Such factors have resulted in innovations which many of the traditionalists deplore. At the festival of 1992 some groups were really play acting rather than performing haka and while this might have audience appeal it has little to do with haka, which has its own conventions.

What many group leaders forget is that the word is far more important than its manifestation in action and movement. Without the word there is no haka and this is the one aspect of contemporary haka that needs serious attention – the language.

Contemporary audiences tend to react to a movement or an action rather than to what is being said and how well it is being said. The language of much of the contemporary haka, particularly those composed over the past two decades, needs to be addressed. The language, which is fundamental to the issue, is becoming peripheral while the actions and movements, the peripheral elements, are becoming the prime focus. With the history of the Māori language over this century it is not surprising that such is the case, but this state of affairs should not be permitted to persist. There should be a ruthless condemnation of incorrect use of language – a mediocre lyric one can do something with for mediocre language can be improved.

There is many a mediocre lyric that has been transcended by the performance of the group. The performance has been of such a high standard that little cognisance has been taken of the lyric. It is fortunate that there are still critics who deplore the elevation of incorrect language use and are prepared to do so publicly. Standards of language as well as standards of high performance need to be sustained but the language must be restored to its position of importance. The national committee needs to assume this important function of elevating the language.

It is fortunate that the impetus with regard to the language is emanating mainly from the young which augurs well for the future. If it were confined to the older generation then one would really have to despair of the language's ever being able to survive.

Haka groups comprise, in the main, young people but there is always a number of more mature performers to provide a balance. Most groups today have performers who are in their mid-teens to those over fifty with the concentration being in the twenty to fifty age group. The older performers with their wealth of performing experience give the group the strength and dynamism so essential to the Māori performing arts.

It is interesting to note that the national committee had decided that the future festivals be festivals, that is, the competitive aspect be removed. However, at the awarding of trophies at the 1992 festival held at Tūrangawaewae, Ngāruawāhia, the chairman of the national committee, the Venerable Archdeacon Sir Kīngi Īhaka, decided to canvass the opinion of all the participating groups regarding the national committee's decision. The groups unanimously rejected the proposal, thus indicating their desire to have the competitive aspect retained. Group leaders and performers are convinced that the high standard of performance at present enjoyed is due to the competitive aspect.

If one considers the marae, one will appreciate that by its very ethic and philosophy, competition is an integral part of the rituals of welcome. Only the best karanga women invite the guests onto the marae and only the best karanga women among the guests acknowledge that call of invitation. These women are the best in terms of their voice, their ability to express themselves imaginatively by making allusions to mythology and proverb, where appropriate.

This is also true of the orators – only the most articulate, the most eloquent and the most learned rise to speak. The chants to conclude the speeches would be performed by those who perform them best and the

84

haka of welcome, the haka to follow the chant, the haka to acknowledge the koha presented by the guests are performed with all the gusto, panache and style that the hosts can muster. The response from the guests is in similar vein because the reputation of both host and guest depend to such a high degree on the quality of performance of all the participants from wāhine karanga to the orators, to the chanters, to the haka people. Even if it is not articulated as such, Māori rituals of encounter engender a healthy competition and the sighs and expressions of admiration are audible to all around the marae.

I have been to tangi where the guests were welcomed with whakatū waewae. The guests also performed a ngeri as they came onto the marae and both were performed simultaneously with each side trying to wrest the laurels from the other although it is always incumbent upon the hosts that they have the final word, that they be seen and heard to be masters in their own domain. This occasion was both an observance of ritual as well as a competition but with the guests realising that their role is to test the mettle of their hosts and to make them look to their laurels. It is on occasions such as these that one hears haka at its most exciting and its most emotional because the context has dictated that such be the case.

Haka as performed in competition like that of the Aotearoa Māori Performing Arts Festival while reaching a high standard will be subject to a rigidity and uniformity that haka performed on marae or at any Māori function will not. Continued rehearsal can do much to remove the more exciting aspects of haka.

It is perhaps the continued rehearsal that is a negative aspect of competition but it is also, rather ironically, the reason why such high standards are achieved and maintained by those groups which dominate the upper echelons of the Aotearoa Māori Performing Arts Festival.

---

[1] Kāretu, Timoti S. *Ngā waiata me ngā haka a te kapa haka o Te Whare Wānanga o Waikato.* pp. 105-106. Hamilton, University of Waikato, 1992.

[2] Polack, Joel Samuel. *New Zealand: being a narrative of travels and adventures during a residence in that country between the years 1831 and 1837.* p. 81. London, R. Bentley, 1838; Christchurch, Capper Press, 1974.

9

THE FUTURE OF HAKA

As seen today on the performing platforms, the future of haka is assured. The young Māori is very much involved in the performance area but has little to contribute to the compositon of the lyric. As stated by Ngāpō Wehi and Sir Kīngi Īhaka, the lyric is the most important aspect of the haka as it is for all the Māori performing arts. The movements, the choreography, the costuming are all peripheral.

If haka is to survive as more than a dance where the performers really do not appreciate what they are saying, or why they are saying it, then greater cognisance has to be taken of the crucial role played by the language. Many haka groups continue to mispronounce words, to use

Vince Heperi

While all these men are performing the same haka, each is expressing himself differently. It is a modern trend to have the performers regimented and uniform in their movements. This trend is because of the dictates of competition, but is to be deplored.

An innovation. The performers in this haka taparahi are using weapons. Traditionally, haka taparahi were haka performed without weapons except for the leader, if he so desired, and the manu ngangahu.

incorrect language and to concentrate on their movements, giving minimal attention to what they are saying. In the final analysis it is the tutor of the group who must take that responsibility and ensure that his language is beyond reproach or that he has access to someone whose language is of the calibre needed.

One can accept that there will be some lyrics that are shallow, ordinary or mediocre, but what they must be is correct. Correct use of language, allowing for poetic licence, is fundamental to the ethos of haka and groups who stray from the principal philosophy must be brought back to acceptable standards. We do our haka, our language, our descendants a disservice if we accept or condone incorrect use of language.

The pithy, acerbic, vitriolic compositions of the past, where much could be said with the minimum of lyric, is now elusive for the majority of the contemporary composers just as the minimum of movement with the maximum of expression is becoming difficult for the majority of the groups to achieve.

Haka will survive well into the next millennium because it still continues to provide a platform for the composer to vent his spleen, to sing someone's praises, to welcome his guests, to open his new meeting house or dining hall, to pay his respects to his dead, to honour his ancestors, to teach his traditions to the succeeding generations. While the language continues to survive so will haka continue to be composed.

Harry Price in *The Royal Tour 1901*, says:

The Māoris call it Haka, it is a kind of war dance, and without a doubt is the best style of savage dancing that one would find, if he searched the whole world over.

The haka taparahi, Tāne-rore, commands us, 'Puritia te haka kia ū, kia ita' but the same haka has a more telling statement, 'Ko te haka he tohu whenua rangatira.'

BIBLIOGRAPHY

Barthorp, Michael. *To face the daring Māoris.* London, Hodder and Stoughton, 1979.

Baucke, William. *Where the white man treads.* Auckland, Wilson & Horton, 1905.

Best, Elsdon. *Games and pastimes of the Māori.* Wellington,⸱ Government Printer, 1976.

Browne, C. R. *Māori witchery: native life in New Zealand.* London, Dent, 1929.

Cowan, James. *Official record of the New Zealand International Exhibition of Arts and Industries, held at Christchurch, 1906-7.* Wellington, Government Printer, 1910.

Dewes, Te Kapunga, ed. *Māori literature: He haka taparahi: men's ceremonial dance-poetry.* Wellington, Department of Anthropology, Victoria University of Wellington, 1972.

Earle,Augustus. *A narrative of a nine months' residence in New Zealand in 1827.* Christchurch, Whitcombe & Tombs, 1909.

Hardingham, John. *The Queen in New Zealand.* Wellington, Reed, 1954.

Hargreaves, R. P. and Hearn, T. J. *New Zealand in the mid-Victorian era: an album of contemporary engravings.* Dunedin, McIndoe, 1977.

Journal of the Polynesian Society. Vol. 84 (4), December 1975.

Kāretu, T. S. *Ngā waiata me ngā haka a tāua, a te Māori.* Hamilton, University of Waikato, 1987.

Kāretu, T. S. *Ngā waiata me ngā haka a te kapa haka o Te Whare Wānanga o Waikato.* Hamilton, University of Waikato, 1992.

Maning, F. E. *Old New Zealand.* Christchurch, Whitcombe & Tombs, 1956. (First published 1863).

Marsden, Samuel. *Letters and journals of Samuel Marsden, 1765-1838.* Edited by J. R. Elder. Dunedin, Coulls, Somerville Wilkie and A. H. Reed for the Otago University Council, 1932.

McKillop, Henry F. *Reminiscences of twelve months' service in New Zealand, as a midshipman, during the late disturbances in that colony.* London, R. Bentley, 1838; Christchurch, Capper Press, 1973.

Polack, Joel Samuel. *New Zealand: being a narrative of travels and adventures during a residence in that country between the years 1831 and 1837.* London, R. Bentley, 1838 Christchurch, Capper Press, 1974.

Price, Harry. *The Royal Tour 1901: or, the cruise of H.M.S. Ophir.* Exeter, Webb & Bower, 1980.

Savage, John. *Some account of New Zealand, particularly the Bay of*

Islands and surrounding country, with a description of the religion and government, language, arts, manufactures, manners and customs of the natives, & c. & c. London, printed for J. Murray and A. Constable by W. Wilson, 1807; Christchurch, Capper Press, 1973.

Sharp, Andrew, ed. *Duperrey's visit to New Zealand in 1824.* Wellington, Alexander Turnbull Library, 1971.

Shortland, Edward. *Traditions and superstitions of the New Zealanders.* 2nd ed. London, Longman, Brown, Green, Longmans & Roberts, 1856.

Taylor, Richard. *Te Ika a Māui.* London, Wertheim & Macintosh, 1855; Wellington, Reed, 1974.

Thomson, Arthur S. *The story of New Zealand: past and present.* London, J. Murray, 1859; Christchurch, Capper Press, 1974.